The
Stop

It might seem strange that opinions of weight
are found in the works of poets rather than
philosophers. The reason is that poets wrote
through enthusiasm and imagination; there
are in us seeds of knowledge, as of fire in a
flint; philosophers extract them by way of
reason, but poets strike them out of imagination, and then they shine more bright.
    —Descartes

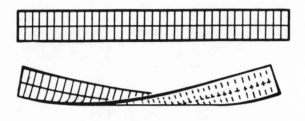

Forming a Moebius strip

Reversal of up and down on traversing a Moebius strip

The
Stop

David Appelbaum

State University of New York Press

SUNY Series in Western Esoteric Traditions
David Appelbaum, editor

Cover: Illustration shows 'Presentation of the Virgin in the Temple' by Titian, reproduced by courtesy of Scala/Art Resource, New York.

Published by
State University of New York Press, Albany

For information, address State University of New York Press,
State University Plaza, Albany, NY 12246

Production by Dana Foote
Marketing by Bernadette LaManna

Library of Congress Cataloging-in-Publication Data

Appelbaum, David.
        The stop / David Appelbaum.
            p.   cm. — (SUNY series in Western esoteric traditions)
        Includes bibliographical references and index.
        ISBN 0–7914–2381–6 (alk. paper). — ISBN 0–7914–2382–4 (pbk. :
    alk. paper)
        1. Vision. I. Title. II. Series.
    B846.A67   1995
    121'.3—dc20   94–48098
                                                                              CIP

10 9 8 7 6 5 4 3 2 1

Contents

Introduction

Now is the time to question the sharp line we draw between fancy and philosophy. Laws of imagination, it is said, are different from those that govern digging in the bedrock of truth. Yet even here fate begets unexpected liaisons and improbable alliances. I am struck by the intrusion of storytelling into a solemn and ponderous logic, when the philosopher suddenly turns to anecdote. A good instance of what I mean comes with citation of an innocuous example. Logically speaking, the example bolsters the argument inductively (by adding its weight to the already existing load) or deductively (by deriving the particular from the general). But the example functions otherwise, in terms of the drama of the argument or the argument of the drama. A character with its idiosyncrasies and destiny has walked across the philosophers' proscenium. He, she, or it is the example. We who as readers see a whole work in which nothing accidental occurs see the example as part of the same story that the main line of reasoning spins. Ordinarily, we are devoted wholly to the chief plot. But if the performance is now regarded through the eyes of the walk-on, then what?

This is the thought by which I would try to outflank a literal-mindedness. A certain example of Descartes's had caught my attention. In terms of timing and personality, it had its oddness even while it seemed to support the main points. What if I saw Descartes's project from where it—the innocuous example—walked across stage? My study was born in this way.

We know from other domains that expression hides its text and that, despite concealment, text finds its way to light through alternative routes. The displaced, understressed, unintended, and overlooked word or deed, in this guise, reveals far more than the famous monologue. Because truth is bent (or we are), the unguarded subtext bears signature of true intentions more clearly than the main body of text does. Read it and you find out what is really being said. There often is play enough to let you catch the conscience of a king.

Descartes provides a text that seems to invite literal-minded thought. But the invitation is a gambit. Fall for it, and you lose the key to the text's inner meaning. Interpreters have been seduced for various reasons. A little foreknowledge is the best defense. I am protected in my investigation by knowledge of this little example, this little walk-on.

The yarn I want to focus on occurs in the deadpan of Descartes's *Dioptrics*. It is the example of the blind man. The *Dioptrics*, Descartes's book on the eye and the sense of sight, is a major work, on his list of credits, just below the *Meditations* and the *Regulae*. For reasons I make clear in what follows, optics occupies a far more central position in seventeenth-century thought than it does today. In this important book, the character of the blind man wanders onstage a ways into the First Discourse, by way of introducing the exalted subject of light. He does little other than illustrate a style of walking but portends much more. He offers himself up to comparisons that bolster the strengths of the protagonist—the one whose eyesight is intact. He uses a prop, his cane. He stumbles across a page and is gone. When he reappears in later scenes, subsequent discourses, he occupies a similar place in the action. He maintains an unobtrusively low profile.

It is the fact he never calls attention to himself that attracts me to him. Similarly, my minor acts, unprepared stagings and impromptu walk-ons, are alarmingly revealing of a character that is mine. There is no time to hide an agenda or sweep the dirt under the carpet. The plot— that toward which the action moves—stands naked and unadorned. This is the moment a philosopher lives for, though too often a little fanciful subterfuge steals sight from it. For there is something in our nature that loves to hide.

My basic surmise in the study is to follow this minor *persona*, this bumbling and unabashed member of the supporting cast, until he leads me to Descartes's real intentions. My *a priori* suspicion, moreover, is that these are provokingly different from Descartes's announced ones. Subtext runs contrapuntal to main text. At least it happens like this when I observe myself and find my real aim at variance with my publicly declared purposes.

The present study is conducted under the usual laws of inadvertence and avoidance. I will nonetheless state my conscious aim. It is to examine a feature of our experience that is most often unwanted, rejected, dismissed, and cast aside. The feature, like Descartes's blind man, makes brief appearances that are always backlit by the star of the scene. To sight it, like a planetary body transiting the sun, one must use a darkened lens. Because of the dynamics of action, it is rarely given its due. Pressures to complete and perfect attainment obscure and eclipse it. Even when it obtrudes into visibility, the momentum of habit and preconception makes observation difficult. In fact, the element I speak of is precisely that which breaks an onrushing momentum and opens experience to another point of view. I call it "the stop."

Descartes's blind man provides a good vehicle by which to approach the neglected matter. His appearance, I have said, is unobtrusive. It threatens no great moment. The sheer weight of avoidance makes an indirect approach mandatory. Otherwise, a monumental resistance to self-examination rears its head, takes precedence, and the stop is secreted away. Besides, the blind man's character—like the gravedigger's in *Hamlet*—exemplifies the very experience sought for examination. In his halting movement across the stage, effortfully groping for a path, laboring to avoid obstacles, occasionally coming to rest only suddenly to lurch again into movement, he impersonates the stop. He cannot rely on the "easy" sense of what lies ahead. He must exert his perception in order to gain the knowledge. In this special species of exertion lies a confrontation with the stop.

I find that the blind-man character holds a radically new understanding of the *Dioptrics*—and Descartes's account of the sense of sight. That the blind man even appears, maintaining a show of his ignorance, his naïveté, his incompetence, is a surprise revelation of its author's intention. When the fact is digested, the real nature of the Cartesian project stands forth. Far from providing a straightforward account of the eye and its visual field, Descartes provides a subtly distorted rendition of sight. He offers it as a token of truth, a sop to our desire for truth. He, like Hamlet, has put on the cloak of reason in order to pursue a more private and duplicitous end. Like Hamlet, he seeks revenge. He has felt himself blinded by tradition and now wishes to avenge himself against the selfsame tradition. And the tradition? It is one that honors sight and proclaims knowledge to reside in the mind's eye. It is one that equates understanding with vision and spiritual perfection with visual clarity.

An innocent blind man provides a clue by which to uncover a plot of revenge? Is this history or a far-flung fancy? Did Descartes actually put on the guise of a Hamlet and set out to make the world anew? Or is this a story "full of sound and fury" that I concoct in order to spice an otherwise bland chronicle?

One thing is for sure. In the domain of text, imagination is king. But a king subject to laws, laws of the story. As soon as one begins the

telling, the costume of storyteller, a most venerable costume, waits.
Anyone who wears the garb bows to the laws of narration. No one can
void a role when it is prescribed by the laws—not the king, not death,
not even God. It does not matter whether Descartes knowingly steps
into a mythological structure that awaits his iconoclastic mood. Role
and text wait to ambush him. Whether he is aware of the machinations
behind the blind-man character matters little. Text reveals what author
is ignorant of—without reproach. Descartes takes on the role of a Hamlet as soon as he sets himself vengefully against his forebears. What follows must obey the laws of mythological enactment.

We have come to a point, it seems to me, of admitting that any
interpretation of text—especially the literal, established, or orthodox
one—tells a story. To interpret is to inseminate what was never invio-
late, to join our energy to a textual form so as to create a new text. Interpretation involves imagination, and so, in a few short steps, mythology.
A science of interpretation on the order of a physics—sleek, rigorous,
and value-free—itself turns on a mythology, an Apollonian one. Once
we admit this, the value of *the* true, correct, or exact interpretation also
grows fictitious. Is a true story the whole truth and nothing but the
truth, or just a story?

The interpretation I offer (the story I tell) is frank heterodoxy or
heresy. An advantage of starting with an eccentric point as center is a
new radius of investigation. Some kind of displacement like this may be
in back of the evolving history of thought and our reach into the future.
Pleasure and usefulness derive from novel perceptions, sure to arise
from a reversal of periphery and hub. New tales rub uncomfortably
against old favorites and often bring suppressed and unwelcome inse-
curities. What I provide might evoke a reaction like this.

Since I speak at length of Descartes's hidden agenda, I want to put
my own on the table. Will that make it any less hidden? It is to reclaim
the sense of sight from its Oedipal blinding, from the blindness it suf-
fered upon our human arrogation of knowledge. Oedipus was punished with blindness because of a fundamental and deeply human confusion. His eyesight had forsaken its embodied condition and had given
its service to a false identity. His eyes failed him in distinguishing the
trappings of a role (king, husband) from himself as witness to his life.
This seems to be the case with all of us. When sight ceases to be related
to its organic condition, it loses its freshness of perception. It fails to
penetrate assumptions we project about ourselves and grows increas-

ingly intellectual—a tendency our philosophical tradition has con-
doned. Tradition accepts the replacement of percept by concept. It
accepts the replacement of vision by thought-construct. It accepts the
result of a blind trust in intellect, namely, that the visual field ceases to
be part of the sensory display as a whole and instead remains detached
from other sense experiences.

My main interest lies in the reversal of this tendency. How can the
eye perceive the suchness of the world? As I understand it, a power that
was stolen or squandered is transformational. Embodied visual perception takes in an impression in a unique way. Not only is a thing unal-
tered (to fit a private intelligence), it also supplies an energy by which
to reveal the context of vision. The progressive refinement of the eye's
function opens a visual field so as to include the one who sees. The
source of the field is no longer hidden from, or beyond the bounds of,
what is seen.

This important development lies at the end of a process of resensitizing sight. An immediate locus of my concern is the start of the process. Engrained habits of disembodied sight give over to fuller, intenser
visual perception. How? In the simplest terms, the first must come to a
stop before the second can begin. The momentum of received visual
learning must be arrested in order for a new (or renewed) function of
sight to commence. The stop, as I call it, defines a center of this study.

No theoretical construct, the stop is an actual moment, the
moment of poise. Dancer, player, and performer display it. But so do
we who pick up hammer, shovel, iron, needle and thread, knife, or pen.
To use an implement with intelligence somehow relies on a gathering
of attention in the moment before we use the implement. An active concentration of awareness—the poise before movement—again is the
stop. The stop lives in the interstices of action, an ordinary recluse. It
shuns the spotlight yet exerts a definite and important control over
what takes place. Furthermore, it gives us a key to a deeper engagement
in a meaning that unfolds our lives. For it offers a choice. Either to
remain habit-bound or to regain a freedom in one's approach to an
endeavor. The stop is the advent of an intelligence of choice.

WHAT THE
EYE SEES

*Since the infusion of grace is very clearly
illustrated through the multiplication of light,
it is in every way expedient that through the
corporeal multiplication of light there should
be manifested to us the properties of grace in
the good, and the rejection of it in the wicked.
For in the perfectly good the infusion of grace
is compared to light incident directly and
perpendicularly, since they do not reflect from
them grace nor do they refract it from the
straight course which extends along the road
of perfection in life . . . But sinners who are in
mortal sin reflect and repel from them the
grace of God . . .*
   —Roger Bacon, *Opus majus*

1

Blindness and Light

Blindness and Punishment

On whom is blinding practiced? Traditional thought contains many instances that share a text. The idea is given in the figure of Samson. In the traditional account, Samson is led away by Philistine soldiers as a result of Delilah's treachery. He is wanted for incendiary acts perpetrated on his enemies. Once he is in captivity, the first act against him—of vengeance and vindictiveness—is blinding. Blinding is an archaic form of punishment. A connection with the *lex talionis* is not accidental. Blinding is the image of retribution, an eye taken for an eye lost. In fact, acts of confinement mimic blinding. They deprive a victim of sight. Dungeon, grotto, tower cell, modern penitentiary all strive to limit the vision of a prisoner. Older forms, modeled on a subterranean cave, actually induce blindness without the act of enucleation. Blinding, the removal of the victim from the light, is repayment for what Roger Bacon called "mortal sin."

Samson is punished not without cause. What are the immediate effects of blinding? Being blind, he is confined. Being confined, he is returned to the confines of his own body. To move forward toward the world, he must stumble to find his way or be led. Action, even a simple act of locomotion, becomes possible only through contact. The idea of action at a distance is self-contradictory for him. Obstacles must be groped around, not effortlessly leapt over. They impress him with their solidity and strength, he who could once hurl boulders at his adversary from a distance of fifty yards. There is immediate payment for perception that is to the profit of action. Blindness returns Samson to the earth, where as a chthonic creature (like Polyphemus the Titan, blinded by Odysseus) he dwells in the cave of his being—no longer god or demigod whose vision traverses the desert in a single bound. No longer can he be raised to celestial heights, to dwell with angelic existence, by the gift of sight. Samson returns to the ground he calls his own—with a question: How to move?

A brief look at blinding teaches why it has been held to be like an expulsion from grace. Blinded, the victim suffers an apparent loss of freedom of movement. To circumambulate the density of things requires a supreme effort. Movement exposes the blind's dependence on a visual impression of location and place, a helplessness and vulnerability in getting from here to there. The blind cease to inhabit a realm of the spatially separate. Things tyrannize and grow overbearing. They hover and loom over the way, threatening encroachment or suffocation. Touch becomes a solace, a primary source of reliability. In this shift, a proximity to things defines the blind. Their manner toward objects becomes reticent and intimate. Things must enter into tactility—an experience of nearness—in order to be known. No longer can the blind command knowledge by decree of separation, remaining physically apart from the known. To know, their flesh must feel the imprint of the world.

Returning to the story, we see how Samson's blinding confines him. The object world belongs to the Philistines (and they to it) while Samson is its slave. His movement, apart from being led by a sighted guided, consists in repetitive action. He performs forced labor, working a gristmill in an endless walk around the same path. He has lost more than his eyes. Becoming a dray, he has lost his humanity.

Blinding adds another factor to confinement: it reduces intelligence. The valuation, ascribed to tradition, is given in the parable of the blind leading the blind. "If the blind lead the blind, both shall fall into the ditch" (Matthew 15:14). In the image of Brueghel the Elder, the fall is all but inevitable. To be lacking in sight is to lack the acumen of avoiding paralysis, derailment, or catastrophe. The Gospel phrase itself is idiomatic for the lowest form of stupidity. To be without sight, led by someone else without sight, is to be dependent on another's thought—a moronic unreason. It is to be an unequal among equals, relinquishing one's responsibility for decision and action. It is to be vulnerable to the abuses of irresponsible leadership. Where independence of thought is the means by which freedom circulates in a democracy of democrats, blinding is undemocratic. As a political act, it throws its victim into a traditional—hieratic, monarchic, oligarchic—form of government.

There is a corollary to the traditional valuation. Blinding reveals the true measure of knowledge. To see things from afar and to navigate with respect to them is to exercise the knowing power. A person of knowledge, hero or heroine, can journey ten thousand miles, avoid death-dealing collisions, and return home safely. One who knows from afar knows the future that looms over the next horizon. This is foresight. Conversely, to know only what is close to hand is to be simpleminded or shortsighted. Distance, a sense of separation, is a measuring stick of knowledge. Nothing is more apparent in the blind's ignorance of the ground—and our own, since the ground often is too close for us to get it into focus and is blurred, confused, and ambiguous. Contrasted with the clarity of an unimpeded line of sight, blind groping is of questionable value. Philosophical method is achieved by stepping back, thereby extending the world beyond our focus.

Once Samson is blinded, however, his thought undergoes a revaluation. His enemies fail to observe a radical discovery of his, that blinding produces no diminution of knowledge. Blinded, Samson comes upon the value of opacity. He is able to hide and feign. Before, his sight, like ours, rendered him transparent. Others could read his intentions like an open text. Now blinded, he grows opaque, a soul in a narrow, dark cell. Therein, his physical strength, mark of his nature, is not diminished, only bounded by his limited circuit. Before, through sight, he could effect changes on objects great and small. His every deed, moreover, could be predicted and foreseen. Sightless, his great body itself comprises a circuit of his force. What he touches, he touches muscularly. In his intimacy, things are molded through respect or awe to the shape of his will. From outside, this might look like a weakening of a prodigious vitality, but it is not. His enemies suffer this confusion. Because of it, Samson is able to work a revenge of the blind. Samson gives us an icon of blind revenge.

Blind revenge is a double action. The blinded act to avenge a punishment. The blinded also act to avenge a peculiar valuation of blinding that the sighted hold. Although there are other cases of blindness in myth, none expresses vengeance as clearly as the story of Samson. Greek myth, to which I return in my conclusion, leaves revenge out of its numerous accounts. Orion the Hunter is blinded for raping Aurora, the Dawn, but eventually petitions his masters and is relieved of his affliction. Tieresias is blinded for revealing Hera's secret love affair, but he is compensated for the deficiency by a gift of second-sightedness. Even Oedipus, who unremittingly suffers his blindness, entertains no moment of revenge in his thought. He accepts punishment as just recompense for his errors. With Samson, however, once plunged into blindness, the discoveries of his state move him from docility to initiative. Blindness has not humbled him. He will not accept that what he knows without seeing is less than what others know with sight. He will not accept an implication of ignorance. Blindness lends a proof the sighted never know. This is the doubled action of the blinded. Samson bends his mighty will in the direction of bringing the sighted into knowledge.

Besides, in the dark closure, Samson actuates capabilities absent in his sighted state. He who was reckless and impetuous is concentrated and contained. He who was accustomed to lash out is patient and all-suffering. There is a wariness that his slavemasters cannot see that leads slowly to cunning. Ignorance becomes an impenetrable mask. To others, he is a bumbling peasant fitting the role of a drudge. To himself, his desire for revenge nurtures dispositions his Homeric contemporary Odysseus is gifted with by birth. Blind Samson acquires wiliness, craft, deceptiveness, and constancy—becomes an Odysseus. With these virtues he works his vengeance. He bides his time. At the auspicious moment, he coaxes a slave boy to rest him against the main pillar of the house. His prodigous strength again revealed, he demonstrates the folly in equating blindness with ignorance. He gives proof that to believe with the eyes is to miss what cannot be seen. The act of collapsing the roof is expressive of the double action. By that act, he ends the enslavement of the blind and begins the ascension of another, more proximate way of knowing.

Gloucester has been brutally blinded. Regan, deceitful daughter of Lear, commanded it. Her royal ambitions overwhelm her compassion, if she ever had any. She dispatches Gloucester to his suffering, shouting, "Go thrust him out at gates, and let him smell/His way to Dover" (King Lear III.vii). Gloucester exits with a single-minded intent, to get to Dover, to "a cliff, whose high and bending head/Looks fearfully in the confined deep" (IV.i). There he will end his sorrow and his life.

The machinery of Shakespeare's dramatics nowhere runs more cogently. Justice is meted out. Gloucester has been blinded because he accepted deceitful affections (from an illegitimate son) and rejected honest ones (from a legitimate son). He is Lear's double, though more transparent to himself. He suffers at the hands of uncompassionate children and is led to truth by his compassionate one. As Gloucester despondently observes, "I stumbled when I saw" (IV.i). Blinded, he must be led forward, like Oedipus, by the human love he disdained. No thought of revenge passes through his consciousness. Like Oedipus, he goes docilely, self-absorbed, penitent, self-pitying. His will, what is left of it after Regan's treachery, is bent on self-destruction. Apparently, he accepts punishment, humiliation, and attributions of ignorance. No Samson of the spirit, he nevertheless faces an immediate problem of the body. If he walks, how is he to move in a world overdense with obstacles?

Yet to Dover he intends to go. And in this, he though hesitant, does not hesitate to seek help. Unlike Samson, he is not driven and so not driven to pierce the veil of ignorance bestowed on him. Gloucester is able to let himself be helped. Even if nobly born, he is ordinary, no archaic giant, but filled with doubt and distraction, like ourselves. His is not the hero's mold, like Hamlet's, who also was cast for revenge. Neither a Nordic nor a Hebraic giant, he calls to us more humanly. If he is no revolutionary like the one who wielded a jawbone of an ass, his quietness commands attention. Though history will not turn around him, his act is a question. How is he able to walk the way to Dover?

Gloucester has entered the labyrinth of blindness. There are no visible signs, except for the dead end, blind alley, or impasse. He feels ground under his feet and air around him, but an object-world has vanished. He could listen, if he had heart to, but strangely that is not an option. Touch, including the sensitive pressure against his skin, is his guide. But touch, foreign to him, is foreign to the way of Western man. It is barely more reliable than the sense of smell that Regan derides to him. Gloucester's movement is stop-and-go, stop-and-go. It is ever ready to respond to obstacles, both outer and inner. It stumbles, it lurches, it staggers. It is awkward and off-balance. There is no pause for relaxation and abandon. When he takes a step, it is because he has found an opening in the labyrinth and dared to enter in.

How can he walk? He dares to pick up the blind man's cane and go.

That he dares is because he holds the golden thread of an Ariade. Edgar, his son, disguised as Poor Tom, takes his hand and guides him through the labyrinth to Dover. Near the crest of the cliffs, below which Gloucester plans to meet the monster and be devoured, his guide stops him. With a noble lie, he prompts Gloucester to jump and lets the blind man's imagination do the rest. When Gloucester revives, he is freed from disquiet and able to resolve: "henceforth I'll bear/ Affliction, till it do cry out itself,/Enough, enough, and die" (King Lear IV.vi). Gloucester can go because he is sufficiently undistracted to follow the solitications of present awareness to walk. His movement is an unmediated act of concentration poised in response to an immediate need: to get to Dover. As soon as nothing is in the way, nothing else is required.

Gloucester's walk is not a question of narrow intellectual concern. It is a deep symbol of a present cultural crisis. We are being awakened to the blindness of our own affections. The ideas of progress, technology, and comfort have preoccupied us. Punishment also, perhaps, but likely more a form of self-punishment, arising from an ill-begotten trust in ordinary sight. We awaken, about to hurl ourselves from a high and precipitous cliff. Just prior to the millenium, we acknowledge the miscarriage of self-destructiveness. We awaken, finding ourselves alone with Gloucester's judgment: "Our means secure us, and our mere defects/Prove our commodities" (IV.i). The importance of responding to the question increases with each step. We lack a guide, unless we can recognize the child we disowned. There is only a walking stick, our hand on one end, the other end probing contact with the earth. It is a tremulous grip on the golden thread.

Descartes's Plot against the Sighted

What does it take for the blind to walk the road? An important clue appears thirty-five years after the first performance of *King Lear* in 1606. Descartes, some time after his revolutionary *Meditations*, becomes intrigued with the problem of vision. Already, he has fit himself to the figure of an avenging hero, a Hamlet. Like Hamlet, he wants to destroy utterly the foundation of things and rebuild it according to a new measure:

> the consequent need of making a clean sweep for once in
> my life and beginning again from the very foundations, if I
> would establish some secure and lasting result in science.[1]

His accomplishment is to be as great as that of another destroyer, Saturn. He would lift the earth from its orbit with his Archimedean lever and establish a new circuit around the sun. The old path is suspect in every detail. Tradition must be doubted if progress is to ensue. "We must read the works of the ancients," he confesses,

> for it is an extraordinary advantage to have available the labours of so many men . . . . There is, however, at the same time a great danger that perhaps some contagion of error, contracted from a too attentive reading of them, may stick to us against our will in spite of all precautions.[2]

Read the old books and then burn them. From the conflagration, a new intelligence will rise and take flight. Self-evident, individual, democratic, perceptive, it will take its place in heaven, along with the Eagle and the Swan of old. In the dawning age, even the fixed stars will be new. And if the stars, then everything else under the sun.

It is some years after the proclamation. While becoming intrigued with sight, Descartes adopts a role that requires a revenge—against views established by his philosophical fathers. In the play of text, dramatic necessity is king. All that Descartes calls his "work" moves ineluctably toward the chosen end. And if the play be the writing of a definitive work on vision, who could the instruments of vengeance, the sword and dagger, not also present? The evil genius of the *Dioptrics* is not its adaptation of Euclidean geometry—wedded to projective algebra—nor its pilfering of graveyards for anatomical data. It lies in the motive; in subtlety and subterfuge, that genius plots to overthrow by distortion and tortuous means. The *Dioptrics* is a work of revenge.

How does the machinery of the eye work? An innocence in the question camouflages the point of attack. Descartes secretly wears the uniform of objectivity while he revolts against traditional accounts of object perception. Their spiritual elitism revolts him. It consists in separating the sighted from the unsighted. Since God's text, elitism argues, is light, the unsighted are without hope of salvation. Since they cannot see, they cannot be seen by divine agency. The sighted, on the other hand, represent the chosen ones, capable of perceiving the visible world and reading the text by which a suprahuman presence reveals itself. Because the sighted alone are agents of moral perfection, the world is bereft of a basis for democracy. For there to be a democratic order to knowing and perceiving, there can be no epistemologically chosen, no noetic hierarchy. Elitism of all kinds must be rooted out and destroyed.

Revenge dislocates intention, diverting it to underground channels where it learns the practice of deceit. Descartes's anti-elitism profits from its subterranean detour. It adroitly attacks that which it appears to support and supports that which it appears to attack. That way, it remains perennially poised for counterattack when tradition stiffens its back. As a case in point, Descartes spends ample time attacking the way intention is traditionally inflected into a mechanics of sight. The butt of argument lies in a denial of "soul" as the agent of sight. "You see," he says, "that sensation does not require that the soul should contemplate any images resembling the objects of sensation."[3] This means that the receptivity of the eye is no higher than that of a windowpane. It assists an impression, not by conscious participation, but by necessities of its nature. The ploy is to offer a mechanics of physiology in place of an ethics of awareness. Elements "by the strength of the disturbance that occurs at the points of origin of the optic nerve-fibers in the brain" compose the perceived impression.[4] Within the process, awareness is a redundancy, an unneeded echo, an aftershock, an "epiphenomenon."

The apparent focus of revolt is against consciousness. That places Descartes among the "new breed" who advocate automatism and habit over attention and initiative. To flaunt his affiliation, Descartes adduces further evidence that the eye is a transfer station. It passively receives a force from outside and passively transmits it to a central processing station. There, recognition, perception, and identification are educed, correctly or not. To this end, Descartes notes that

> if you observe that people hit in the eye think they see a great number of fiery flashes in front of them, in spite of shutting their eyes or being in a dark place; this sensation can be ascribed only to the force of the blow, which sets the optic nerve-fibers in motion as a strong light would do.[5]

Time and again, he empties the eye of special intelligence and leaves it a dutiful machine. The eye does not bodily participate in the impression and add its own light to the incoming illumination, as tradition once had it. Descartes undercuts this view:

> As regards position . . . , our knowledge of it does not depend on any image, nor on any action proceeding from the body, but merely on how the minute points of origin of the nerves are situated in the brain.[6]

Like Hamlet's, moreover, Descartes's skill is subtle and duplicitous. As with guerilla tactics, the apparent locus of attack is diversionary. Descartes attacks what he wishes to defend and defends what he wants to annihilate. When done, he deploys an account of sight that poses as a tasteful advance of traditional work in the field. It is in fact an act of Odyssean cunning, a Trojan horse that unsuspecting workers will appropriate, to their dismay. The *Dioptrics* seems to advance a project that began with Euclid and Ptolemy and passed through Alhazen and Al-kindi to Kepler. When inspected more closely, however, it is a text that renders sight, insofar as it belongs to the body, unthinking and unthoughtful, degenerate and blinded. It is an account that empties sight of its function—of relating humanity to the unseen cosmos—and fills it with objects, commodities, bibelots, bric-a-brac, trinkets, and other worthless things. Where the eye once felt gratitude for resting on the sights of heaven, sight, in Descartes's version, now serves its master as a clock does, without affection or awareness.

I have not yet shown the means, but it is testimony to his genius that Descartes accomplishes his end. Great reversals—making the lower the higher, and the higher the lower—occur. After him, sight becomes blindness, and blindness, sight. No longer is blindness a "darkened" vision, a sight with the lighting rubbed out. Henceforward, vision is enlightened blindness, a deprivation of sight with light added in. Sight in fact becomes an addition that is a subtraction, a step backward that is constantly trying to make up for its fundamental lack—the blindness that is its core. Sight becomes anxiety, grasping, a nervous reaching beyond for what is no longer there, a something wrapped around a void that no beauty or truth can erase. Sight becomes our flaw, a symbol of the fault of humanity. Was not Oedipus redeemed through his blindness? To see, we must be blinded.

Yet this is no ending suited to a vengeful tale. That other remaker of tradition, Hamlet, rewrote his own death warrant while on a sea voyage, and Rozenkranz and Guildenstern were killed instead. He had time for other grand reversals, including a metanoia, before revenge cost him his life. That revenge against revenge, that dropping of the avenging hammer, showed him through the portal to a compassionate vision. Whether Descartes ever comes to know an understanding heart is a question beyond the text. Like Hamlet's, however, Descartes's intelligence is devious, determined, and distracted. He camouflages his impulse in order to seize the power of sight and overthrow it in its inadvertency. Like with Hamlet, his ineffectual reason in the end betrays his purpose, leaving his original project broken and in ruins. Yet there is a little more to Descartes's tale than this. It is the small addition that I mean to dwell on. For as Descartes dons his disguise, he makes a dis-

covery that radically revalues his world. His discovery is of an element
so insignificant that it is continually lost, yet his discovery is so monumental that it shakes the revolutionary ground he stands on, over-
throwing both insurrectionist and establishmentarian alike. This
incomparable discovery is still hidden from us in the same way it was
for Descartes. It is hidden in the undoing of ego consciousness. I speak
of Descartes's unheralded discovery of the stop.

Descartes's Revenge

In the drama, Hamlet's motive of revenge makes an early appearance.
His father's ghost disturbs the peace of the night watch and the minds
of men who sleep. Horatio first bears witness to it. The initial move that
brings resolve to Hamlet is a swift one. That this initiation itself falls
under question is part of Hamlet's greatness. From *Hamlet* to the *Dioptrics* is a few short steps. Looking to the *Dioptrics*, in Descartes also, we
are quickly met with a motive of revenge under cover of night—though
the dramatic element is suitably muted, even subterranean. Themes of
darkness, blindness, and absence of sight, coming at the opening of a
treatise on vision, might alert us to the author's hidden agenda. If they
do not, we may at least question the choice of such a method of
approach. To understand the phenomenon of sight by studying the
blind is an idea as outrageous as studying corpses to understand the
phenomenon of life. That is precisely what Descartes the physician does
in his anatomy.
    Listen.

> It has doubtless some time happened that you were walk-
> ing across difficult country by night without a torch and
> had to use a stick to guide yourself; and you may then have
> noticed that you felt, by means of the stick, the objects in
> your neighborhood, and that you could even distinguish
> the presence of trees, stones, sand, water, grass, mud, etc.
> True, without long practice this kind of sensation is rather
> confused and dim; but if you take men born blind, who
> have made use of such sensations all their life, you will find
> they feel things with such perfect exactness that one might
> almost say that they see with their hands, or that their stick

is the organ of a sixth sense, given to them to make up for
the lack of sight.[7]

The program apparently accomplishes in one fell swoop Descartes's
radical revision of (read, *revolt against*) tradition. It makes blindness the
primordial condition. In support of the claim, blindness is our state *in
utero.* We enter the world, after an initial journey down the birth canal,
with eyelids tightly drawn over our organs of seeing. Blindness henceforth becomes the archaic situation by which study is compelled to ori-
ent itself when determining who we might be and where we might be
going. To accomplish his end, Descartes must to put on the cloak of
blindness and move on.

It is a condition of extreme constraint. Blindness's impediments
are real and enormous. They include lack of discrimination, dimness,
vagueness, obscurity, confusion, and animal sensation. Movement of
any kind meets resistance. From place to place "across difficult country," movement, as we saw with Samson, throws a traveler back onto
the field of immediacies. What is directly in front of me? How do I navigate toward and around it? What threatens to destabilize my motion?
On what ground do I stand? For a blind traveler, the route across
appears only at the very moment of stepping onto it. It preexists on no
map, plan, or chart. A traveler must pay close attention to proximities
and contiguities. One is not free to participate in the play of intellect,
imagination, or the higher mental powers. Success depends on a single
condition: one remains a slave to the demands of navigation.

In the context of a study of vision, to try on blindness is a tactic
of disorientation and dislocation. The sighted enter into another world,
of the unseen obstacle and hidden barrier, a dark encounter that is
costly. Their apparatus of locomotion meets traps, quagmires, sandpits,
and mudholes. It gets entangled in the very act it seeks to accomplish.
Compare the world of the sighted. Sight removes all impediments.
Once they are visible, the pitfalls that lay hidden in the distance of the
world become harmless. Danger announces itself before the wayfarer
becomes bodily ensnared in it. Separation buffers the threat of object
density. It gives the luxury of deliberative reason, to choose between
alternatives prior to meeting them. Sight discloses visual space that, to
all appearances, is spaciousness itself. By enveloping everything, it
allows that which it contains to stand apart, one thing from the other.
When *with* but *apart from* the contents of space, the sighted run less risk

of collision, unexpected turn, or catastrophe. To be able to see before stepping: that is the blessing of sight.

Descartes hopes to displace the sighted by plunging them—following him—into blindness, but a small surprise of great magnitude awaits him. He dons the cloak of philosophical blinding and stumbles ahead, "walking across difficult country." He falls, gets up, loses himself, falls again, is hurt, and gets up again, paralyzed by confusion. Though driven by impractical and impracticable demands, he nonetheless heeds the call of practical reason. There is need for a guide where none apparently exists. In the momentary return to his humanness, Descartes stops, bends down, and picks up a stick. Henceforth, he in his blinded state will have use of the blind man's cane.

This is a great moment, a moment of true discovery. A giant breakthrough, it ends a paralysis of the blind and opens them to movement in the human journey. The blind no longer need be fixed in place nor give over slavishly to a seeing eye, to be led from place to place. They are instrumented with a new dignity that overcomes handicap and constriction. They are handed skillful means to seek and uncover the things of the world. Stick or cane equips them for movement essential to full humanness. Cane swings from side to side until stopped by an object. In that stop, the blind attain full perception. Through perception, Descartes grants them the power of locomotion. The stop of the cane resurrects the blind from the abyss and sets them on the road to Dover.

An unforeseen and unforeseeable reversal occurs. In the stop comes a reversal of revenge and an end to blinding. In the stop, the blind find direction, continuance, and hope. Vengefulness itself is an unknown god, bearing an unknowable gift. It is a gift too magnanimous for Descartes to acknowledge. About the gift, he remains forever mute. The gift? It is the gift of poise.

Poise is a balanced concentration immediately prior to action. It is the a priori of a self-aware act. Poise itself is an action, but one of a wholly different kind. It differs from ordinary undertakings in point of origination, intention, quality of attention, rhythm, and reason. Poise is the response of awareness to the call of a situation. Dancer, athlete, player, and performer—as well as we ordinary agents—all embody poise. Poise becomes attentive to the needs of what is in front of the actor, and so becomes poised. Poise is ever fresh in its ability to answer to the forms addressing it. In its continually renewed sensitivity, it is unlike its apparent siblings—control, steadiness, and firmness of intent. Poise has flexibility. It stretches, bends, adapts, and accommodates while the others remain fixed. Thus, poise is friable. It does not break or shatter in the face of a rapidly evolving confrontation. Poise is fluidity of response.

Fluency in response announces the advent of a new factor—or perhaps an old factor hidden within the springs of ordinary action. On closer examination, poise is a radical break with an ongoing, unpoised mode of doing things. Before poise can reveal itself, a tension that is the psychophysical milieu of accomplishment must ease. Tension obscures poise or banishes it to the ideational realm, where it becomes the idea of relaxation or relief. Tension is a context. Its primary subtext is that of trying to figure out, plan, and engineer outcomes. The subtext is Cartesian (and pre-cartesian) rationality working away in its blindness to the needs of the actual situation, afraid of failure, doubting its own methods, and racing to prove its self-worth as time runs out. The subtext is cluttered with overabundant information and impoverished by an absence of real facts. It is frenetic, overworked, disquieted, and imbalanced. Within a context of tension, little chance exists that a call of the actual situation will be heard.

We must not conceive of poise growing out of a moment of tension as a flower grows from a stalk. All evidence suggests that poise is not a natural outgrowth of a process that begins in distraction, preoccupation, and insensitivity. From that context, only hyperactivity and disharmony result. The dancer's jump is too rigidly placed, the athlete's application of strength is poorly timed to coincide with his shot, the actress's lines sound mechanical or inappropriate to the occasion. Or, in more ordinary circumstances, we miss our chance to get through the revolving door without mishap, to step on the escalator, to hit the platform running as we disembark from a moving train. Bad timing is the mark of unpoised action. In fact, to act without poise is always to act "out of synch," to miss opportunities to meet that which the time offers, and, so, to tempt fate. It is to collide with the shifting door rather than to pass through into the flow of action. About this, I will say more.

Poise is no natural outcome of distraction. We may, therefore, deduce that a transition to poise brings closure to the context of preoccupation and despair. One comes to an end, the other opens. Between closing and beginning lives a gap, a caesura, a discontinuity. The betweenness is a hinge that belongs to neither one nor the other. It is neither poised nor unpoised, yet moves both ways. It is this space that is the primary subject of my interest. It is the stop.

There is a moment in which personal or cultural history stands before two diverging pathways. One leads to a repetition of the known, the tried and true, the old, the established. It is safe, secure, and stale. The other finds a renewed importance in the unknown, the uncharted, the new, the dark and dangerous. Unfettered by accepted categories of thought, it might be immediately hidden away from view, out of fear or repugnance. The moment I speak of is not choice in the sense of deliberative reason but an action that choice itself stands on. That action is awareness. Awareness confronts the line between engaging in or becoming disengaged by what follows. Awareness is an addition that multiplies distinction. With respect to action, it brings a moment of supreme importance. The stop is the time of awareness.

The stop hides in a most hidden place. This is a place that is both near and obvious. As if being of the same polarity, our habits impel the gaze toward what is distant and complicated. To gaze is in fact to look far off, toward the unapproachable, the not-at-hand. It is a look of dissatisfaction, peering behind, around, in back of, rather than directly at what is in front. It is an averted look. The habit is of ignoring the call of the personal, cultural, and human. It runs very deep.

Western thought early developed an aversion to the stop, because to stop is, among other things, to confront the aversion. Not to stop, to race through a context cluttered with priority and instrumental means, means to abhor a vacuum, a gap, a hiatus. Such abhorrence has been a driving force behind thinking since classical times. In its customary fashion, thought codified its aversion into a universal law in order to secure more protection against the stop. That what lurks might hold up a mirror to the self and its fears and desires is a repugnant possibility. Under scrutiny, thought would face its subtext from which it flees—the fact of avoidance. The stop reveals habits of escape of intellectualism.

Greek thought, the first mask archaic experience puts on, offers a good example of how the stop is barred from thought. In both Plato and Aristotle, the circle represents perfect movement. In Aristotle's expression, the perfection of circular movement lies in its continuous and uniform (= ceaseless) motion around a point. Such motion is celestial, embodied in heavenly bodies that revolve in their orbits. A circle is thus heaven transposed into the human realm. The lengthy astronomical exposition of circular movement, until Kepler's discovery of the elliptical orbit, attempted to preserve perfection in the face of recalcitrant facts (such as the eccentricities in planetary motion). As above, so below. If heavenly orbits remain circles, then their earthly correspondents also must exhibit unceasing, uniform motion. Departure from circularity must demonstrate an incompleteness, a nonbeing, a not-yetness. All terrestial motion that is noncircular indicates a lack or absence. All that fails to fit the agenda of circularity is ruled void. The stop is opposite to uniform, ceaseless motion. Hence, it is excluded from the text of motion.

Yet the stop is ubiquitous. The stop is evident in each and every earthbound action we experience: shoveling, hammering, opening a door, using a pen, eating, driving, running, lifting, skating, swimming. All involve a joint. There is a hinge around which events pivot. An initial impetus to movement runs its course and is followed by a new impetus leading to a new movement. All earthly movement is a deviation from perfect continuity in that it stops, begins again, stops again, hesitates, recovers, moves on, stumbles, falls down, gets up, crawls ahead, trots, gets sidetracked, lopes along, slips, gets up again, and so on, to the end of its drama. All motion approaches unimpeded, effortless motion as a line approaches an asymptote—in perfect mental (= celestial) space. In the space of phenomena, all motion is imperfect.

The text of the daily round is intellectually reinterpreted in order to avoid disclosure of the stop. The function of the rational automatism is precisely here. The attention is repeatedly, ceaselessly, and unknowingly given over to an onrushing stream of associative thought. Habits, dreams, assurances, secret fears, cherished beliefs, and hopeless infatuations—together with their objects—are therein perpetually revalidated. At no time is notice taken of a gap between two thoughts. The smooth rational function annihilates the pause by which real and unreal come under question. An endless automatic movement of thought obscures the stop.

What is ceaselessly perfected is a history of erasure. What is ceaselessly erased is a space between one occasion and the next. What is responsible for erasure is an unchecked, automatic movement of one thought following another following another. The virtual movement of the automatism replaces a real arrest between ending and opening, between death and birth. As long as there is no stop, there is no time. This is the secret to thought's immortality.

Descartes's Stop

The stop hides behind a facade of unimpeded, effortless motion. The appeal of Aristotle's circular orbit lies in the perpetuation of conceal-ment. Although many correspondences to circularity exist, for my pur-poses it is important to study one, that of vision. Once the eye is opened, sight continues ceaselessly and without apparent effort to renew itself. It leaps instantaneously across the valley to the mountain on the opposite side. Sight does not stop even as the scene undergoes slow or rapid change, from night to day, from lightning flash to dark of storm. It continues uniformly and without apparent gaps. It neither hesitates nor falters nor stutters nor stumbles regardless of a resistance it meets in its object. Once the eye opens, sight, the noble sense, is the very perfection of perpetual motion.

In the modern era, verification of sight's perfection was given at about the same time as Kepler discovered the imperfection of the celes-tial sphere. Kepler removed perfect circular movement from the heav-ens. As a compensatory adjustment, at least equally important, visual perspective in the graphic arts happened on the scene. Once discovered (or rediscovered) by Brunelleschi, perspective—the precursor to Des-cartes's own projective geometry—was a representation of perfected (= unimpeded) vision. The eye's visual power extends outward without surcease, never coming to the end of the visual field even when most distant corners of the cosmos become visible. Perspective in the visual arts is a vehicle for ceaseless, effortless vision. Its projection of an infin-ity, a dimension of depth and distance that is strictly illusory, expresses an ideal, not a real motion. A horizon, infinitely distant, seems to be the natural call toward which an unimpeded line of sight travels. The prac-tical proof that sight is able to move to infinity is in fact deceptive. Hori-zon, line of sight, and projected infinite all belong to the same subtext that is perspective. The infinity perceived is the one contrived by the rules of perspective.

The greatness of the discovery of visual perspective may be mea-sured in its effectiveness to conceal. Any momentary arrest in the move-ment of the eye in relation to spatial contour has been rendered invisi-ble. Perspective, after all, is an illusion, and the magnitude of an illusion lies in what it protects. The greatest illusions conceal what is nearest and most obvious, the subject taken in by illusion. To stop is to become aware of the awareness in its subjectivity and objectivity. The invisible guidelines a perspective artist erases allow the eye to travel without stop. The stop thus hides the one who waits hidden in unchecked movement.

Let me return to Descartes. His traveler has set out to study sight, the noblest of senses, and the subject of perspective, but suffers from a bad case of night blindness. Relying on what is only a privation, he stumbles across rough turf. By a stroke of genius, provoked by necessities, he picks up a stick. When he walks again, he walks guided by the stop.

In the arrest, perception is altered. It sharpens and is subject to finer discriminations. From this position, Descartes notices another movement, more primal than that of the halting, lurching pitch of his body. It occurs, mediated by a stick—the blind man's cane—*within* his body, within the fleshy folds that by means of a hand grab on to one end of the stick. It reveals a something the eye does not. Descartes struggles to comprehend. He compares the event to the disclosure of sight. It is like sight in being able to distinguish one thing from another. It is like sight in allowing one to navigate around the obstacles of the way. It is like sight in being used to perceive, conceive, imagine, and opine. But it is not sight. It is another mode of perception.

Also, it is unsightly, almost beggarly, how this other perception proceeds—in several ways. It cannot be confused with sight, because it is start-and-stop in its action. Its rhythmic movement bespeaks a meeting of resistance with effort. Unlike sight, the unnamed perception belongs to a text of effort. It makes no instantaneous leap to celestial bodies. If one looks closely, though, the stick differentiates neighborhood objects, it is more keenly sensitized to that which is other than any thing in the milieu. It perceives an undifferentiated background from which objects arise (when disturbed by the tip of the stick) and to which they return (when tip passes over). It perceives nonobjectively.

There is another important way in which the other mode of perception is not to be confused with sight. It eschews life in ignorance of the stop. It can no more avoid the stop than it can provide material for its own perception. The blind person's cane comes back, over and again, to the arrest, the gap in perfect motion, the hinge between one event and the next, and there finds poise. Poise is its way to initiate movement to contact what is. Contact defines the path of the blind.

The blind are unable to escape the unavoidable. Therein lies effort and the fruit of effort. They were thought cursed by a deficiency. Instead, it is their blessing. To return to the theme of revenge, the springs of Descartes's plot derive in part from the purity of the blind. Through revenge, Descartes engineers a series of startling reversals. Blindness ceases to be God's punishment for sin and becomes a reward for meekness and service. The blind, unlike the sighted, are truthful. The sighted, unlike the blind, are prone to oversight, lying, escapism, and withdrawal. To have a seeing eye is to be damned. To turn a blind eye is to open oneself to a heaven on earth.

Yet the blind must work. It is no Eden they inhabit. They must earn each and every perception, and when they go slack, they fall quickly into a ditch. They are proletarians of awareness. The object of desire is never guaranteed them in the way that sight fixes an object, holds its position in space, and lets the seer approach to grasp it. The blind find it necessary to work against rigidiy, fixation, and conceptualization. The blind must grow mistrustful of stagnation if they are to survive. It is their relentless but secret pursuit of movement that makes them despicable to the sighted. It is their acceptance of imperfect movement that renders them outcasts. They are hated because of their ceaseless probing and questioning of their immediate position. They are objects of hate because they remind us of our forgetfulness.

It is consistent with Descartes's strategy that he downplays the work of perception. His aim, it must be remembered, is to present a plausible, attractive, but false view of how sight works. In a convoluted manner, he strives after the downfall of spiritual elitism and the rise of a new age of intellectualism. Thus he writes:

> True, without long practice this kind of sensation is rather confused and dim; but if you take men born blind, who have made use of such sensations all their life, you will find they feel things with such perfect exactness that one might almost say that they see with their hands, or that their stick is the organ of a sixth sense, given to them to make up for the lack of sight.[8]

The blind become upright by virtue of an ennobling practice. They practice in order to perceive. Blind perception takes on the yoke of practice. It is a yoke the sighted will never willingly wear. They will not willingly relinquish the ease and security by which they maneuver about the world. For that ease is a protection. Their embrace of security is prompted by a fear the uncertainty masks.

Fear, moreover, is another mask. It is as near as the light switch. Turn off the lights. Bring sight to a stop, and attention is returned to another, forgotten movement. Turn from the object world, from the known, the clear, the distinct. An undifferentiated sensation appears "dim and confused" to an unpracticed perceiver. Confusion habitually provokes reactive emotions, notably fear. The reactive configuration stands as an obstacle to a moment of poise. It is what must be met to become responsive to the needs of the situation. Poise results from a return to a state of global sensation after letting drop what stands in the way. Poise is an abandon that revitalizes. It is the space of a breath.

Herein lies the work of awareness so much despised by the sighted. It is a work of return to the habitat of an unsighted perception. The return is to an organic, archaic level of experience. It is a return from a constructional, conceptual mind that predominates in the daily round. The return involves dwelling in the body as awareness while face-to-face with entrenched impulses to take flight. It is a practice in the sense of remaining unperfected, never unceasing, always needing to begin anew. Its imperfection is why the blind man stumbles.

The Disanalogy

Remember that Descartes has an ulterior motive when he recommends that we

> conceive of the light in a 'luminous' body as being simply a certain very rapid and lively movement or activity, transmitted to our eyes through air and other transparent bodies, just as the movement or resistance of the bodies a blind man encounters is transmitted to his hand through his stick.[9]

Though he seeks revenge, the plot falls short of his final object. The ways in which it misfires I will examine below. Its misdirection, however, does not stem from a lack of planning. Descartes's strategies for success are impeccable. Instead, he fails because of what lies beyond his control, the discovery of the stop. Its force, the force of novelty, breaks the forward momentum of his project and leaves him needing to regroup.

Descartes fails to take into account the stop hidden in walking blind. The blind man's cane swings forward and hits a rock. Wood reverberates with the force of impact. Vibration is transmitted to the grip of the blind man, who registers a shift in the field of his tactile experience. By analogy, light striking the rock should vibrate "air and other transparent bodies" that vibrationally affect the eye. There should be a corresponding shift in the field of visual experience. But here the analogy comes to its limit. "Luminous" vibration leaps across an ethereal gulf to the eye that receives its unimpeded movement without a vibrational impression. There is no gathering of "dark vibration" such as the blind know. No activation of the proper receiving organ takes place. Seer need not attend to present sensory experience at all. Sight, in fact, is colored by a curious inattentiveness.

The analogy's failure is patent, but Descartes camouflages it. It needs to fail, moreover, because it cannot distinguish two kinds of receptivity. If it did distinguish them, it would discern a receptivity of awareness—and this, by Descartes's machinations, is not allowed. He wishes to present a mechanistic view appealing enough to topple tradition. The view must supplant the former elitist presuppositions with ones thoroughly democratic. Mechanism, in counterdistinction to consciousness, supports the impulse to democracy. Hence, the cosmic clockwork proposed by Descartes: "The only difference I can see," he says,

> between machines and natural objects is that the workings of machines are mostly carried out by apparatus large enough to be readily perceptible by the senses . . . whereas natural processes almost always depend on parts so small that they utterly elude our senses.[10]

In the Cartesian universe, each event takes place automatically, by laws of indifference, that is, cause and effect. It is important to make note of the roots of the obsession. Perfect and unalterable causal functioning is yet another subtext written by the same hand that devised circular movement and perspectival drawing. In that text, the infinite is perfectly ceaseless. It never need come to a stop. An unerring clockwork guarantees perpetual motion. Its work depends on making irrelevant the vagaries of will and consciousness. These factors alone are capable of influencing a process in the direction of an arrest. Rule them out by framing suitable laws of the cosmos, and events run smoothly forever. Epiphenomenalism is the genius of this mania.

The causal universe is another triumph of the view with which Descartes seduces his opponents. What is set in motion abides forever in motion. What is at rest is stuck there forever. This is the realm of angels and absolute inertia. Strangely, angels lack will and consciousness. Being conservationists and maintainers, they are perfectly obedient to that which they serve and lack their own intentions. They ensure continuation of what is but can take no hand in aiding what might become. Because they can brook no deviancy, they are incapable of acts of self-transformation. They are endlessly what they are, in perpetual movement around themselves, in orbits that allow no eccentricity or personal acceleration. They, like causal agents, do not live in time, and if they have an action in time, it is distant, indifferent, and without purpose.

To watch the progress of Hamlet's revenge is to feel what a hesitant instrument intellect is. Cut off from the body of action, its plots misplay, its launchings are delayed, its planning is excessive and obsessive, its quiet nil. The world continually fails to conform to its thought. Only when it falls into the gap, during Hamlet's sea voyage, is mind opened to that which encloses intellect in its warm, vibrant embrace. Though I have not written the play of Descartes's revenge, it must go quite like that. And what he finally brings off, like Hamlet's act, accomplishes so much more than his original end, but at great personal cost.

After all is said and done, the modern aversion to blindness is not very different from the classical aversion. Each deploys a different strategy. The classical solution involves the negation of arrested movement I mentioned. The modern one involves negation of an arrested awareness. The two are not very different in their denial or in their affirmation. It could be said that because the stars and planets go around in their perfect orbits, the angels need exercise no discernment. So too for us moderns, who aspire to be angelic.

A Postscript on Berkeley

The circle drawn by punishment and revenge needs no completion. It is closed from the beginning. The blind were punished and blindness was their punishment. They were blinded because they were offensive to the eyes of the sighted. Through their punishment, they came the reason for the vindictiveness toward them. As it turns out, the blind were punished because they ceased to avoid the stop. They were punished because they, having come face-to-face with fear, were feared. We also, in coming to a stop, meet a fear that is there to meet us.

The stop hides a secret dimension of experience. To stop is to uncover what is in hiding, which is to say, to experience ourselves in hiding. Yet the stop means more. The stop opens and closes. It opens to an actual unfolding of a life event, that which lives on the other side of the hiding. To come *to* experience is always to come *from* a disembodied, disengaged state of thought construction. The first is the unhinging of the second, and the stop is the hinge. The stop is not the negation of movement. It is movement itself, a form of movement purer than that of body, mind, or feeling alone. It is movement away from entrapment in automatic and associative thought, just as it is movement toward an embodied awareness. The stop is a movement of transition.

Concealment of the stop—concealment of experience itself—is the mind's devotion to conceptualizing activity. Although it is present in classical views, mentalism finds a new faith in modernity. Mentalism is responsible for an increased blindness as to how we are to negotiate the way to Dover. Upon taking a Cartesian turn, a mind grows ineffectual in challenging an indifferent universe that indifferently thrusts ruts and stones in the way. It ceases to be interested in the steps of the journey. What attracts it is the look of its own operation. From this inquiry follows the self-infatuation of our modern tradition. Narcissus remains blinded by his beloved, his own reflection in the lustrous waters.

Almost one hundred years after Descartes, Berkeley takes up a study of sight. The premises of vengeance are firmly in place. Berkeley will unhesitatingly accept the starting point that sight is a kind of illuminated blindness and work from there. If the eye, he will reason, is in reality not open to the world, it therefore cannot see. Yet it is undeniably the case that as we walk along the road, we are guided by some power, some ability. That power cannot be sensory nor bodily nor organic in origin, since body in itself is mute, dumb, deaf, and mindless. It must, Berkeley, concludes, be the mind itself that lights up the way. It must be the mind that sees through blind windows of the eyes. It must be intellect that discloses a world through its radiant operation.

This is a diabolical development. That not the eyes but the mind sees impoverishes sensory content in visual experience. It also reduces the exercise of sight to comparative judgment. Nothing fresh enters into an act of seeing, because seeing consists wholly in comparing a current tableau with past ones. Seeing is seeing sameness. Seeing is the same seeing the same.

On Berkeley's recommendation, the optic apparatus could be replaced by blank glass or a corneal lens. No quality of receptivity is intrinsic to it. That sight is a product of conceptual processing means— as in all processing—that one kind of raw material can be substituted for another *without loss*. One kind of sensory input may be used in place of another—sound, taste, or touch can be used in place of sight. None presents the different; all present the same. Perfect interchangeability holds among the senses. Thus blindness is a punishment that is no punishment at all. No new content is sacrificed in blindness, since nothing is new in sight (or any other sense) that cannot be gotten elsewhere. Being blinded is being returned to a condition where conceptual processing must discover another source of material—a far lighter sentence that Samson bore. Berkeley is like Heraclitus's infamous pupil who dared outdo the master, arguing one could not step into the same waters even once. Berkeley has outdone Descartes.

In addition, Berkeley argues that concepts or "ideas" relating to sighted experience have evolved with the help of sight. They are both its products and its templates. Anyone speaking the mother tongue has access to them. The blind see no better nor worse than we do. They see without being disadvantaged by an actual deprivation of visual impressions. They see the way the sighted see—with seeing thoughts.

There is one anomaly to Berkeley's correction to Descartes. The blind know the stop. They know the stumbling, groping way they walk the earth. They know the effortful experience of uncovering the shape of the world through bodily contact. They know the paramount value of the data of difference. How will they be with the unfolding of a reality that leaps with the speed of light across to the other side?

Berkeley writes:

> a man born blind, being made to see, would, at first, have
> no idea of distance by sight; the sun and stars, the remotest
> objects as well as the nearer, would all seem to be in his eye,
> or rather in his mind.[11]

"Distance by sight" does not correspond to how the blind travel. Perspective, the virtual third dimension, a visual portrayal of depth, does not yield the blind's experience of distance. Distance, for them, is fragmentation, dispersal, distraction, imprisonment, separation, captivity.

The distant is what they are cut off from. They feel a lost connection and lack means of rejoining. The distant is coldness and despair. The distant is hopelessness and helplessness. The distant is indifference.

This is a most uncomfortable discovery. Berkeley feels the discomfort and tries to smooth over the anomaly by pointing out that visual habit must be learned. But the discovery cannot be suppressed. The blind do not see the same as we, the sighted, do. They see difference. They know the stop. "Hence it follows," Berkeley confesses,

> that a man born blind and afterwards when grown up made to see would not, in the first act of vision, parcel out the ideas of sight into the same distinct collections that others do, who have experiences which do regularly coexist and are proper to be bundled up together under one name.[12]

Even if the blind learn habits of sight, they do not entirely forget the terrors of the way. The distant is no figment of mental imagination. The irrepressible, incomparable, absurd element that appears when thought processing comes to a stop is their existential guide. It is neither calm nor predictable nor patient nor welcoming, and they, like Gloucester, do march under its command. One false step, one moment too long detained by an associative judgment, and the abyss swallows them.

2

The Ceaseless Agony of the Blind

Samson's Body

With each of the Samson icons—Gloucester, Oedipus, et al.—there is impetuous, destructive action that follows a trajectory of punishment by blinding, discovery in the milieu of blindness, and, finally, revenge. The slewing of Philistines with the jawbone of an ass is mirrored in Gloucester's arming of King Lear and in his exploding at Regan, both incendiary acts. Blinded, Gloucester uncovers a discerning heart and eventually a strategic revenge against his perpetrator. Even where the icon is incomplete or distorted, wild, self-destructive action supplies the keynote. Oedipus wanders into Thebes and ascends willy-nilly to the throne, vowing to rid the country of brigands and murderers while he himself is one. With the icon, the sloughing of a tenacious vision, like an old skin, proceeds violently in order to expose both a new receptivity and an avenging spirit. Where the icon has been modified, as with Oedipus, the basic composition remains, with the revenge motif transmuted into penance, a kind of vengeance against self.

When the icon has been intellectualized and made transparent, its meaning is more manifest. In the case of Hamlet, violence is directed against sameness, the sameness of a man imprisoned by habits of inaction. Hamlet wants to destroy his uncle's illicit reign, but only by wild, inconsistent action is he able to break the stranglehold of procrastination. What is the same is his mental habit, its expository, analytic mode perpetually replacing the drive to action. For Hamlet, to act would be to encounter difference. Descartes, cast as a Hamlet, wants to raze the foundations of old ways of thinking. That he wants to rid the world of sameness, a world grown insensitive to the upsurge of a new individuality, goes without saying. Sameness is an impediment, *the* impediment, to democracy. Democracy works only with difference, diversity, and a plurality of things known and perceived.

27

Both intellectualized types suffer a similar kind of blinding. Both are blinded by doubt and indecision. Hamlet's blindness is involuntary. He cannot see his way to action. Descartes's is a kind of voluntary and experimental blinding, ingenious in the way it turns the very forces that subjugate—doubt and indecision—to his own end. Like an unsuccessful gambit, the strategem breaks down the walls of tradition and the cosmic order they protect, only to install a "new" system that is more of the same. So much for the icon's surface grammar. Its depth grammar moves in contrary ways. In this act of injury, I have said, lie the hidden seeds of a truly different order.

The lesson of both Hamlet and Descartes is that of any Samson icon. To crush the visible order in the millstone of change results in disorder and death and not much else. In Descartes's case, the thought of "I," the *arche*-name, the self, replaces the interrelatedness of beings on all levels. But it is a mere thought, still veiled from an experience of individual existence. Like all thinking cut off from its organic context, it lacks a vitality with which to cultivate and actuate difference. Even as Hamlet gains a surpassing understanding, at his death, war drums announce the chaos engulfing the kingdom. Hamlet has avenged his father's murder only to enthrone a new usurper. How can the same give rise to difference? Only when the wheels of change grind to a halt does a Hamlet or a Descartes engender a new order.

This much is true of Samson himself. Samson, the icon of a blind giant pulling down the temple of earthly order, himself is crushed by the order of change he ushers in. His discovery is born in his death. He is part of an old order that must be superseded by what is different. He must die. In his death, moreover, one order comes to a stop. Another is not yet started. In the new, the discovery unearthed by Samson's death is about to be rediscovered. The Samson icon is an image of the moment of transition. In transition is the hiddenness of the stop.

In a text of change, the Samson icon is a punctuation mark. It separates one subtext from another. Any punctuation mark is a timing device. It signals a change of text and controls the rate of transition. One needs to know how to read a comma, semicolon, or period in order to decode the timing belonging to a transition in text. The icon contains the secret of timing. The importance of the secret is that it enables its holder to act in harmony with the tempo of change. Without the secret, there is only a blind encounter with influences through which change is manifested. That is our ordinary way of action, more of the same. The secret is contained in blind Samson's poise as he grasps the collapsing columns. In the concentrated form before action, he comes into contact with his intention and task of being. Only through contact is his action in accordance with the times. Only through contact is his act in harmony with what the times dictate. Only then is he free. The secret is the secret return to poise before contact.

The matter of timing is crucial. To walk through a revolving door at the wrong time is to meet with intransigence, inertia, or injury. Collision with an obstacle disables the endeavor. Hopefulness falls on barren ground if timing is off. To find a gap in the revolving door of habit, subjective necessity, or "gentle custom" requires exquisite timing. An unpoised attempt frustrates by confusing an agent with questions of doubt or self-worth. In the poised stillness of blind Samson, we find something quite different. The Samson figure remains agile while awaiting the inevitable moment of achievement. It gives itself over to an active readiness, banishing all thought of expectation and consequence from its mind. This quietness, far from being a weakening, is a Samson's strength. When novelty arrives, the fact of its novelty derives from another level. The act expressing its arrival is not more of the same but is actually different. What Samson is poised to receive is not another conceptually processed surrogate of experience. Instead, his receptivity is directed toward an order of awareness.

In the original icon, the most impressive aspect is his physical strength. Milton has Samson speak of "this high gift of strength committed to me" (line 45).[1] This aspect is preserved in Orion and later distorted in Samuel Beckett's character of Pozzo. The icon's presence is felt as a physical one. Its importance needs emphasis when understanding the relation between timing and a new order. The secret Samson receives comes through his body. In the poise that brings him to an awareness of who he is and what is being asked of him, he comes to a consciousness that inhabits his body. This is the essence of novelty. Samson's experience is of an embodied awareness. It is an advent he awaits in order to usher in the waiting world. This is Samson's revenge.

The crushing of the habitual and mechanical, even as he crushed grain in the gristmill: this is Samson's achievement. It is achieved through good timing and awareness of the stop. The stop is a hinge between heaven and earth, awareness and the body. When it is swung one way, awareness becomes disembodied, disjointed, and disenchanted. When it is swung another, the body becomes mindless, reckless, and dispirited. When it is hinged properly, body and awareness, joined, reveal a way of working in harmony. This is the disclosure of a new force in creation. This also belongs to Samson's achievement, an achievement crushed by the selfsame act that announces it.

Poise is the return to time. Blind Samson at the pillar is a man returned to his body, to corporeal existence. Inhabiting his organic fold, he no longer is a "thinking substance" but one that resonates with environmental tempos affecting him. His is a temporal existence, which means a tempoed one. As his hands grope to press the column, he gropes in his hands for the pressure of the attention. To accomplish this feat, he must occupy time present. The way time pulses in his fingertips is in tempo with the way it pulses through his whole body. Samson has returned to time from space that is separation, from distance that is indifference, cause and effect, dispersion, multiplicity. He has returned to the simple unity of life in time, in accordance with time, life no longer divided by divisive desires, thoughts, and projects. He is ready to trumpet his discovery to the Philistines.

His discovery reveals that poise is the moment or measure of time.

Samson Agonistes

Regarding the question of Samson's revenge and its secret moment, Milton, the blind poet, writing in 1671, raises the following question:

> Since light so necessary is to life,
> And almost life itself, if it be true
> That light is in the soul,
> She all in every part, why was the sight
> To such a tender ball as the eye confined,
> So obvious and so easy to be quenched,
> And not, as feeling, through all parts diffused
> That she might look at will through every pore?
> (lines 90–98)

This is a new question. One may suppose that Milton's mortal condition drew him to examine the Samson icon from depth of sympathy. One may further suppose that his own experience led him to question the sharp opposition of sightedness to blindness and even to ask about the *seeing* of the sighted together with the *seeing* of the blind. In the revolutionary times with which I am concerned, the development is important and new. Descartes's revenge was to make sight a mechanical but "illuminated" blindness. Milton's triumph is transform blindness into an unsighted but soulful seeing.

Milton's is a serious reexamination of traditional attributes of sight. A carefully constructed argument is provided. Sight, we saw, was held to be the classical model of perfection in organic human experience. Its perfection was spatial and temporal. Its gaze upon the infinite provided a window onto eternity and infinite distance. Sight's character of endlessness—the angelic panorama it enjoyed in looking out over all created things—was manifest in the way that the seen was effortlessly present to the eye. Visible things were present without exertion and persisted in that condition unless eclipsed, occluded, or otherwise removed from a field of vision. The thing seen was seen in duration, since the thing was perfectly enduring.

Yet an aspect of perfection is apparently missing. Sight is not omnidirectional and ubiquitous. As an example, Milton cites "feeling" as arising everyplace at once and entering a field of perception as though "through all pores suffused." Feeling comes from nowhere and is felt everywhere. Feeling is, as perfection requires, omnipresent.

Feeling is an ambiguous term. It can refer equivocally to emotional life or to sensate experience. Both emotions and sensations share in a quality of ubiquity. We do not ask which body locale experiences joy or hope or where the sensation of exaltation is found. Fear may grip the pit of the stomach or envy constrict the chest, but neither stomach nor chest is properly speaking the site of feeling. Some sensate experience is localized. It corresponds to a superficial level of the organism. A sensation of a numb finger or a scraped elbow happens in a definite place, as do other pains, aches, itches, pangs, or spasms. The superficiality of feeling is expressed by its lack of perfectability—those qualities of omnidirectionality and ubiquity Milton points to. Perfectability of feeling, in short, refers to being perfectly available to perception.

Put another way, feeling's perfection lies in the special property of the "organ" of its perception. In order to perceive the global character of feeling, the organ itself must be global. It must not be confined to a simple locale. If it were, like certain pain receptors are, its particular perceptions would be of the surface and not the depth of sensate or affective experience. Such experience would be of relative, not universal, validity.

When we consider the organ of sight, the eye, certain facts are obvious. Sight takes place when light passes through a small aperture, the pupil. Photosensitive nerves in the retina respond to visible radiations. Close eyelid over pupil, and sight comes to an end. Place the eye so that visible radiations are absent, and sight does not function. Damage the receiving apparatus, and sight is no more. That an experience of sight depends on the intact nature of the eye brings into question sight's exemplary perfection. Everything might not be as perfect as it looks.

Just as the smallest twitch of the hand under a microscope appears gigantic, so too the slight revaluation of sight causes enormous movement on the moral plane. Sight is no longer perfection. Other orders of experience begin to emerge from the shadows of that sense. Because both light and dark conceal, they also reveal. The oppositions, sighted/blind and light/dark, suddenly no longer form a perfect rectangle. In fact, they no longer form any rectangle at all. Blind Samson is not thrown beyond the pale of light, into eternal darkness, the "dark, dark, dark, amid the blaze of noon" that he laments. Under the revaluation, blindness is a fixity. Being blind is being fixed in darkness, being fixed, period. The blind are blind because they cannot move, the way feeling moves throughout the global expanse of the organism. The blind are blind because they are stuck.

A new aspect of the Samson icon is thereby illuminated. Samson is not only blinded. He is imprisoned. He is confined in his movement to a narrow cell in Gaza. His ability to enter into movement is taken from him. The millstone to which he is chained has a peculiar construction. To work it, he must go around and around in a circle. The circle in the Samson icon, far from being the template of perfection, is the prisoner's chain. Dull, endlessly repetitive, desensitizing exertion: this is to walk in a circle. A circle imprisons one in necessity. It is impossible to strike out in a new direction. Everything known is worn and stale. To go around in circles is to be stuck. The circle in the icon is also Dante's icon. It is a circle of hell.

Samson's agony is real but concealed by an outmoded text of darkness. Without sight, unable to move, he is an exile from time. Adrift from time, he cannot act in accordance with what there is for him. Not being in tempo with influences acting on him, he remains locked in opposition. He cannot undertake an aim in harmony with the times—whatever the times might be. That Samson cannot help himself is his agony. That he is cut off from who he is is his agony. And that his plight is eternally, endlessly the same is his agony.

Thus, Samson "Agonistes."

The eye's gaze is traditionally held to represent the acme of its perfection. The staring, unblinking open eye whose constancy equals that of the world *sub species aeternitatis!* Let us look at the wide, staring eyes in Titian's *Presentation of the Virgin in the Temple*, painted a century before *King Lear*, in 1490. If humans had such eyes as the painted figures', they, like those of a fish, would be lidless. Thus does the fish become symbol of a perpetual, uninterrupted seeing.

Titian's work portrays many attitudes: incredulity, hope, scepticism, belief. The proud stand beside the disgraced, the generous are with the niggardly, the rich with the petty and thieving. But regardless of character and disposition, the eyes of all gaze with equal rapture. The lids are vestigial. In that frozen moment when the young woman mounts the temple steps, they gaze with a gaze that will reach no end, neither in time nor in space. It is the gaze of eternity, fixed rigidly, repeatedly expressing the same thing, not changing in accordance with changes in the times. The contemplative figure in red regards the visible world with constant receptivity, unswerving in the face of his affective or sensate experience. What alters in him in the unfolding scene is no more changed than is the distant mountain by a passing cloud. He is a fixture, an architectural element, a manikin, an anatomical specimen.

In gazing, we come closest to the angelic realm. In the gaze, nothing that passes in front of the eye causes an interruption. The reflexive dropping and raising of the eyelid that so much marks our mortal frame is a prime source of a broken gaze. This temporary darkness when the world is shuttered out might serve well to reveal the signature of our state, but it is for the most part erased. Our habits of sight do not reveal momentary gaps but one seamless web. Only a careful examination or a chance dysfunction shows that the visible world darkens and then, a split second later, is relit. A discontinuity caused by the blink has vanished.

If the world blinked off and on like a firefly, and we were found to suffer from chronic, intermittent blindness, great insecurity would abound. A kind of active oblivion comes to our defense and redraws the visual field. Thought is at its service. Thought is so arranged as to posit enduring and permanent objects. They remain what they are—thought says—even though our sight is repeatedly and unremittingly broken. The gazers who watch the young woman ascend to the Temple elders see one continuous reel, not several starts and stops. Thus, what they watch, it must be said, is not their actual experience of what takes place but an idealized version of it. Their care is not for facts and phenomena but for their careful, subtle revision of them. The revision posits permanence.

The first lie of the gaze concerns the blink.

The second lie of the gaze concerns its fixity.

In the gaze, the interocular muscles do not move. The eyeball itself is locked in orbit. It ceases to shift right and left, up and down, as while taking in an impression. Fixed on an object, it is undisturbed by organic or affective events, local or global. Nor do peripheral matters alter its fixity by their calls for attention. In the gaze, the visible world has become macular. It has been defined in a central focus, cut off before edges blur. The visible world is like a field at the far end of a paper tube, a sudden tableau emerging from a chaotic, undifferentiated penumbra.

In the gaze, sight holds itself to be higher, more refined, than in unfixed eye movement. Gazers are the chosen, the elite, those with talent and leisure enough to engage in an endless look, an uninterrupted use of the eyes. Elevation in this context originates in pure rather than practical reason (Kant), intellectual rather than moral virtue (Aristotle). In either case, the milieu provokes no impulse in the gazer and thus ceases to be an influence. In the present instance, the onlookers at the Temple exhibit no inclination to shift position, flex their muscles, and navigate the world. They are, like the fixed stars of the empyrean, at perfect Aristotelian rest. To gaze is to be a celestial spectator removed from the springs of action. With the look unbroken, continuous, without a terminus, distraction shrinks to zero. In the bloodless eye and bodiless vision, indifference replaces engagement. Perfection of the gaze lies in never abandoning heaven for the sake of earth.

The gaze lives beyond the pale of action. There, fixity coincides with passivity. A separation in our humanity takes place. The gaze is unable to blend contemplation and action, seeing and doing, organism and intellect. The gazers at the Temple represent so many "thinking substances," so many mechanical (though angelic) reactions to a scene visually before them. In their disembodied, starstruck poses, they do not belong to a realm of action. Action is perpetually deferred. Action is a tangent, an arm casually pointing at an object or resting on a shoulder of a neighbor. It is the difference to which those who gaze remain indifferent. With the gazers, action has been removed, absorbed into a higher power, as from a stone statue.

But the gazing eye appears luminous and full! This is the illusion of its art. In reality it is void of human intent. It is an eye not yet human.

To grow human, it must embrace its organic terms. It must grow trusting of the intermittent darkness that falls over its light. It must blink.

Detachment of the gazing eye renders it indifferent to the field of action. But we should not conclude that the organism, or its agency, is the sole locus of indifference. Indifference is far more global. Uncaring, the gaze feels no sympathy with what it sees. Lacking common ground with what the gaze falls on, the gazer sees only the gulf between self and field. In the separation, looker confronts looked-upon as subject confronts object. An object is something in the way, an occlusion, an eclipse, a blockage, an undesirable, a problem. The gaze is the object-making eye, the eye of objectification.

Look at the faces in Titian's work. Eyes stare out of holes in immobile masks. Self-possession, confidence, and composure color the faces of the onlookers. Vulnerability, insecurity, and desire have all been banished. The changeless shows forth where once the changeable played. Is this not the mark of the perfection they live in? Look more closely. The gaze is itself a mask. It is a physiognomy frozen in place. It serves as a protection against surprise—the unpredictable, the absurd. The gaze is held in place by a series of replacements. Vacancy replaces spaciousness. Timelessness replaces timeliness. Pose replaces poise.

Immobility of the gaze is a replacement for fluidity of poise.

A Digression on the Gorgon: The Look That Slays

The Medusa icon supplies a text of replacements regarding the gaze. It can be read accordingly. Medusa was a Gorgon who, along with Stheno and Euryale, came to life only in night light, starlight or moonlight. Darkness was her milieu. In full light, her glaring eyes were blind to objects, though she was perceptive through other senses. To those with eyes to see her in daylight, she was of notorious ugliness—serpents for hair, huge teeth, a protruding tongue, and a face that petrified those who gazed upon it. Her face had a look that froze the look of anyone caught by it and robbed them of their life. In this way, Medusa was able to protect a secret in her possession.

According to the story, Perseus sets out to slay Medusa and bring back her head as a condition of marriage. He is aware of the difficulty of a frontal attack. Meeting with Athena, known for her strategic imagination, he learns of the Gorgon's secret. He also accepts a present of a brightly polished shield. In addition, he acquires an adamantine sickle, a magic wallet, winged sandals, and the helmet of invisibility—a formidable batch of weaponry. Perseus arrives in daylight and finds Medusa asleep. She is surrounded by the stone figures of those who tried to approach her face-on. He holds the shield at arm's length, locates the mirror image of her on it, and lifts the sickle. The neck is severed, and, still looking in the shield's image, he drops the head into the special wallet. The prize is his.

What does the icon say with regard to the gaze? Medusa possesses a kind of night vision. Her eyes cannot fully accommodate to well-lighted conditions. In order for her sight to function in dimness, moreover, she must—like us—abandon her use of focal vision. Focal vision locks in on an object by differentiating it from an undifferentiated background. The visual field is then organized in terms of drawing forth the object. The line of sight from the visual center to the horizon relates focus and background. Perspectival drawing recapitulates the discovery in the unimpeded way the eye passes to the horizonal infinity. The object is brightly lit, identifiable by the "primary qualities" that give it form, such as shape, size, and weight. Being identified, it is accorded the status of a permanent resident of the world. At the same time, it is made different from all other such residents. It may also have other, secondary qualities, fine flourishes that complete its unique portrait.

The Medusa is a creature who must surrender her focal vision in order to gain sight. She must rely on peripheral vision. When the eyes defocus and attention moves from the macular region to the periphery, the visual background emerges from invisibility. In contrast to the foreground, it is penumbral. Its presence can be seen, but no distinct forms, contours, or shapes emerge from its dim lighting. It is that which abides when an object stands forth. Whether it remains the same or is in flux is a question. Likewise, whether it is empty or full of contents cannot be directly answered due to its lack of particular qualities.

The Medusa's secret lies in her impairment. It is a secret handicap that contains a secret. She has no focal vision, no means of distinguishing objects. Lacking a straight-ahead view, she can see only by looking away from the line of sight. Her glimpse is an averted one. Her sidelong glance takes in what there is in front of her. For her to confront this face-to-face is to see nothing—to be blind. Medusa's secret is that she sees along a deflected line of sight. Her vision is bent.

The secret of sight along a deflected line is important. In the secret is both a power and a vulnerability that Athena divulges to Perseus. A deflection is a stop. Sight with a deflection involves an arrest of the unimpeded, ceaseless movement of focal vision. A line of sight no longer stretches endlessly to infinity, but twists and turns, suffers partial reversals, comes back on itself, bends and rebends, and is at each deflection arrested in its stubbornly forward direction. It relinquishes its indefinite extension and accepts the condition of sublunary vision. No longer avoiding the stop, Medusan sight moves with it and is vitalized by it. Energized, that vision commands supernatural power, power to stop the life of those who approach it. It has the power to kill.

The power of Medusan sight can, however, be neutralized. To look in front of her, she must look along a deflected line of vision. Another's gaze meeting hers directly is stopped and stripped of its life force. But what about a look that is also itself deflected? What about a look that incorporates the arrested movement and demurs on the effortless seizure of infinity? When Perseus picks up the shield and watches the Gorgon through it, he does just that. His line of sight goes out, is stopped by the reflective surface, and recovers itself in an altogether different direction. It is thereby immunized against the Medusa's superior force.

The Medusa icon contains the secret of the gaze. Like any icon, the information it contains has a universality beyond the situation portrayed. The secret is a double secret. The first secret is that to turn the gaze outward is to run the risk of being turned lifeless. Being able to turn to stone—the Medusa's power—means having perceptions of stone, cold, unreceptive, closed. In stone, there is no movement, no exchange, nothing organic. A heart of stone lacks feeling altogether.

The second secret of the icon concerns a revitalization of the look. For sight to have and maintain a perceptual energy, it cannot express itself through a direct gaze. To gaze directly is to give over to habits of effortless perfection and infinite extension. It is to abandon the terrestial for the angelic. Such habits take us outside of ourselves, outside of the fine tissue of a perceiving organ sensitive to the life of the moment. They leave us distant from and indifferent to the question confronting us: Is the confrontation exhausted by the object?

Sight along an indirect line implies a return to a concentration of form before action. Perseus lifts the polished shield and beholds the sleeping Medusa. He has not passed helter-skelter to the act of lifting the sickle from where it hangs at his belt. Nor does he abide in merely looking at the Medusa in a remote and philosophical manner. He stops and recollects his aim. He allows a space of readiness to alert him to what is to take place. He grows sensitive to the time and what it requires of him. With poise, he follows the movement of his weapon from his side, higher and higher into the air. . .

Poise is the secret Perseus gains from Athena. Poise is what the Medusa face steals from its victims, returning gaze for gaze, turning them to lifeless stone. Knowing her strategy, Perseus is not to be unhinged from his place in time. Meeting her deflected look with one of his own, he is able to call on his resources of the moment. No nervous faltering draws him into her gaze. Not wavering, he dispatches the threat to his life and intelligence.

The Cartesian Geometric

Samson's agony is to live cut off from time, from the energy flow of his life source, from a harmonious relation to his own nature. Blinding does not bring about this condition. The source of Samson's agony is his atemporal existence. His gaze is continually directed toward the timeless. Being made blind throws him back to immediacy, physicality, and hope—to "this strength, diffused/No less through all my sinews, joints, and bones" (line 1140). Blinded, he can no longer be victimized by the Gorgon gaze. His flesh is not transmutable to stone—or, in terms of a more modern technology, to pigment on the canvas. A way of discovery opens for him. It is a return to the tempo of action through a connnection with his organism.

Samson ceases to be geometric. Geometry lays out a measured and universal expanse to replace the particular ground actually walked over. The local is replaced by the abstract: number, line, and spatial coordinates. Geometric vision is another twist to Descartes's revenge against the sighted. To tempt his followers away from the traditional account, he replaces a lived vision—replete with ambiguities of overlap, superimposition, occlusion, inclusion, interpenetration, and contiguity—with the trompe l'oeil of perspective. Felt depth, its lack of and longing for contact, is replaced by imaginary lines that create an illusion of a depth dimension. A real movement into and through a foreground is replaced by a virtual movement along ingeniously constructed objects that arrives nowhere. What is the great attraction of art over reality? An elimination of the stop and the indeterminacy of time. Unlike those with whom the Cartesian strategem works, Samson opts for uncertainty.

Descartes's revenge against sight involves a similar displacement of the body. On a canvas, space is the container of bodies in relation to one another. It is the relation of relations. Titian's *Presentation of the Virgin*, we saw, contains bodies of onlookers in relation to architectural structures, all related by the pictorial volume of the canvas itself. If we think of a specific body as that which occupies a definite space in the canvas, we arrive at Descartes' definition. "The nature of matter, or of body considered in general," Descartes writes,

> does not consist in its being a thing that has hardness or weight or color or any other sensible property, but simply in its being a thing that has extension in length, breadth, and depth.[2]

The brilliance of his plot lies in making the craft of perspectival drawing definitive of body itself. Body becomes drawn space, "visual space," a space of orthogonal and horizon. A newly spatialized body has length, breadth, and depth, but lacks any of its temporal aspects, rhythm, pulse, tempo, syncopation. Conveniently, it can be geometrized, mathematized, and quantified without loss. This convenience eliminates a lingering threat to the timeless, ceaseless mode his vengeance purports to install in power. Geometric space never comes to a stop.

There are further strategic advantages of Descartes's elimination of time from the inner relations of bodies. Time is extrinsic, so organism, soma, and corporality "in general" are suitably studied after life— that which is so intractably temporal—has left. A fledgling medical science takes a giant step forward, following Descartes's lead, through its dissection of corpses. It is part of a wider movement the wedge of geometric spatialization creates. A burgeoning science of the external world seizes upon Descartes's act of vengeance and builds a hegemony over older, traditional branches of knowledge. An individual prospective drawing is made up of numerous points, each unique. Each may be numbered and the bodies occupying them thereby rendered distinguishable from all other things. This is a return to Platonism with a vengeance, a metaphysically blinded Platonism. To help usher this in, Descartes further declares, "Quantity differs from the extended substances, not in actuality, but only as regards our way of conceiving them; just as number does from what is numbered."[3] The bold identification rapidly becomes the manifesto of the new order.

Just as sight replaces other senses, and blindness, sight, so space replaces time, and number, space. The system of replacements emerges with the emergence of an ethics of indifference. Such an ethics reaffirms its essential passivity. A passive ethic has a weak attractive force, one that will be repulsed by a stronger attractive force of the ethic Descartes keeps hidden. A passive ethic is ripe for insurrection. It has ceased to be aware. The cessation of vigilance is one of Descartes's objectives.

Samson waits in readiness. Look back at him. Samson is not indifferent. He has passed from indifference to action, destroying in himself the remnants of geometric vision. He has ceased trying to see like someone with eyesight and has embraced the seeing inherent in his blindness. Samson has grown kinaesthetic. "When our blind man," Descartes writes regarding his accompanying diagram (see fig. 1)

> of whom we have already spoken so much, turns his hand A towards E, or again his hand C towards E, the nerves inserted in the hand cause a change in his brain, and this enables his soul to know not only the places A or C, but also any other places lying on the straight line AE or CE; he may, e.g., turn his attention to the objects B and D and determine their places without in any way having to know or think of the positions of his two hands.[4]

A blind man's hands see. There is no effortless leap by which gaze bounds from eye to object to foreground to horizon to background and

Figure 1. The blind traveler, after Descartes.

back again. Sight, which is ineluctably drawn toward to an infinite horizon, is no more. Teleologically, as Bacon said, the eye is made to gaze upon heaven. When there is no eye, one must walk the earth and find another way to the stars.

Why not question the look heavenward? A cause of gravitational attraction to boundless extension may lie in the vicinity of what is close up. When the near and proximate are felt to be undesirable, the eye looks evasively into the distant horizon. The ready-to-hand falls conveniently out of focus and, like a background, may be disregarded. An attraction to distance comes as a solution to a problem. The problem is that which lurks in immediacy, its undesireable character waiting in ambush. The solution is to evade the context from which sight arises. It is to rewrite the text, setting the distant equal to the important and erasing the near.

Descartes's suggestion that the blind man can walk "without in any way having to know or think of the position of his two hands" gives another solution, one Samson knows. To turn his attention to objects B and D, he must attend to his own two hands. This requires a stop. Its achievement requires that an automatic look into the distant and infinite horizon be arrested, and the momentum of framing experience in concept and thought must be reversed. An arrest of intellectualization allows an awareness of a different order to arise. Old, discarnate habit yields to time and immediacy—conditions for novelty. In contact with an inner surface of the hands, Samson is able to know, by means of an intensive measure, the objects in his path. A new relation to sensate experience guides him. He is in a position to reject Descartes's outrageous statement that "we do not perceive the nature of anything by sensation alone."[5] Samson has entrusted himself to a different intelligence and surrendered the scheme of projective geometry to the Philistines.

At the same time, we need to read Descartes's disguises with extreme care. Having put on the mantle of blindness, he works his vengeance against the sighted. Yet the disguise is not perfect. To see through it involves acknowledging that the blind can walk the road. Their organic awareness might be hidden from sight, but its results are not. Descartes might further disguise the awareness by stressing the results of perception and ignoring the process itself. Perception thus reduced would be concerned solely with outcome, success, achievement, attainment, its measure always the same: Has an object been identified as such? But he cannot keep suspicion entirely away from the sensation of hand and arm, even though that experience fails to produce objectified results. The groping effort of the blind to return through awareness to an organic and sentient habitat stands out as an obvious fact. It evaporates Descartes's smokescreen of "sensations representing nothing outside our consciousness."[6] We see again Descartes's dilemma. The cover Descartes needs to preserve—the inferiority of the blind—is blown by granting them the power to walk along the road. As they go, they perceive through sensation. By their very walk, they defeat his strategy. *"Ambulo, ergo sum."*

Introducing Perspectiva

Descartes's plot—Samson's revenge—is furthered by an unlikely accomplice. Relying on her popularity and the impeccability of her reputation, Descartes is able to cover some difficult ground. With her help, a geometrization of sight is completed. The eye no longer sees what it does not create. All independent checks with reality are surrendered and vision is exhausted by illusion. Though Descartes does not us tell this, his agenda is clear. It is to usher in the age when the eye ceases to bear the scepter of moral authority among the senses. Who is this fair spirit, this ally on whom Descartes can depend in his battle against the usurping tradition of the spiritually elite? She is none other than the genteel *Perspectiva*.

Human affection is fickle, and this one's hour has passed and is now forgotten. But a century before Descartes's ruse, she was one of the presiding muses. Her name was on the lips of the learned and the wise. Extolling sight, Leonardo mentions her in his notebooks:

> The eye is the master of astronomy. It makes cosmography.
> It advises and corrects all human arts. . . . It is the prince of
> mathematics. . . . It has created architecture and perspec-
> tive and divine painting.[7]

About the same time, in the year 1493, the Florentine artist Pollaiuolo casts the bronze tomb of Pope Sixtus IV. This was to lie in the church of San Pietro in Vincoli. In the allegorical relief, Perspectiva is included, along with the trivium and quadrivium, as one of the liberal arts. She is the eighth art. She displays an open book in her right hand. The pages are inscribed with phrases from John Pecham's *Perspectiva communis* (c.

1265). Who is this mysterious figure who reclines on a divan at the side of notables such as mathematics, music, and philosophy?

Medieval *perspectiva* was an important science that drew together theories of perception, optics, and optical anatomy amid a growing fund of empirical observations. It was not only an important science, but the most fundamental of natural sciences. Of it, Roger Bacon would write that

> it is necessary for all things to be known through this science, since all actions of things occur according to the multiplications of species and powers from the agents of this world into material recipients; and the laws of these multiplications are known only through perspective.[8] [*Opus tertium*]

The unlikely collection of disciplines comprising perspective was assembled for a single purpose: to explain how the eye saw what it did. Aristotle and Plato, Euclid, Ptolemy, Galen and Avicenna, Al-kindi and Alhazen were some of the workers in the field. Three English Franciscans, Grosseteste, Bacon, and Pecham, each made significant contributions to the metaphysics of sight. Pecham's book accomplished an important synthesis of geometric optics and led to the experimental research of the Arab Alhazen. *Perspectiva* flourished, moreover, while other disciplines waned, since it was buoyed by an eminently practical set of interests. Controversies within it were closely followed by artisan, artist, and architect. For them, the dialectic between appearance and reality was no theoretical matter but one of their livelihood. To build or to paint required an artist to know how the eye would see the result.

The achievement of Pecham's book, building on Grosseteste's and Bacon's thought, was a great one. It opened a view of optical rationality and offered a precise (= geometric) model by which God diffused his grace across the world. Light, the primal divine work, connects the unmanifest with the manifest. Pecham shows how optical principles allow understanding to penetrate the mystery of the universe even up to absolute darkness. Sight becomes geometry's servant in adoration of the *lux gratiae*.

By Pecham's time, three central issues of *perspectiva* were apparent: the causal explanation of sight, the geometry of the visual field, and the metaphysics of light. Different issues occupied different theorists. First there was the question of what caused the experience of sight itself. Since Greek times, two views vied for authority: (1) intromission theory, which maintained that all visible objects give off *eidola,* or films that somehow impregnate the eye's surface with the object's shape, size, color, and composition; and (2) extramission theory, which claimed that our sight works, in Al-kindi's (after 870) words, that

> [2] by power proceeding from the eye to sensible things, by which it perceives them, or [3] by these two things occurring simultaneously, or [4] by their forms being stamped and impressed in the air and the air stamping and impressing them in the eye which the eye comprehends by its power of perceiving that which air, when light mediates, impresses in it.[9]

Other possible theories are (3) a combination of intromission and extramission theory, and (4) the mediumistic model of Aristotle and, as we saw, Descartes. Whether (1) or (2) was found adequate had to do with whether an active or a merely receptive role was assigned to the eye. It was not until Kepler, who wrote the *Paralipomena* some thirty-seven years before Descartes published his *Dioptrics,* that the theory of the retinal image—a version of intromissionism—resolved the dispute. From Kepler on to our time, the physical eye was deprived of an active (intromissional) place in the visual field.

The second matter—of grave importance to *perspectiva*—is the geometry of the visual field. Euclid is an early contributor. His *Optica* attempts to derive principles of sight by the same axiomatic method successfully used in the *Elements.* Euclid's is an extreme reduction of sight to geometry and one from which thought today is unable to shake itself entirely free. Of the *Optica*'s seven principles (from which follow the fifty-eight propositions), the first two have special importance:

> Let it be assumed
>   1. That the rectilinear rays proceeding from the eye diverge indefinitely;
>   2. That the figure contained by a set of visual rays is a cone of which the vertex is at the eye and the base at the surface of the objects seen.[10]

The first permits an analysis of the visual field solely in terms of straight lines. It thereby leaves the entire realm of the visible susceptible to a geometric approach. The second is even more radical. It locates the place from which all sight issues. The observer is situated at the farthest extreme, the apex, of a cone constituting the visual field that ends with its object. One point more distant and the observer would stand outside, looking in. From Euclid's innovation, it follows that the sighted are, by virtue of their sight, near outsiders, that they are on the brink of not belonging to the field of vision, that they are connected to the transactions of the field by the slimmest of points, that they are marginal. Nor is this conclusion metaphorical, any more than geometry is for Euclid. The eye's near exclusion, its peripheral relation to the visible world, is much more than a diagrammatic convenience. It describes the way things are. From Euclid on, the eye will pay the price of being exiled to the farthest corner of the illumined field, a mere speck on the conical surface of the visible.

Another ancient geometrist, Ptolemy, adds an important feature to Euclid's work. While for Euclid visual rays that fan out from the eye have equal value, Ptolemy argues that those nearer the center of the visual cone are shorter. The impression they convey is therefore clearer and more precise. The centermost ray, or *axis visualis* (as Alhazen is to call it), when perpendicular to the object, is clearest of all. The effect of this corollary is to value macular or focal vision at the expense of other portions of the visual field. Surfacing gradually, the prime consequence of the valuation is a selective attention. Brilliant illumination of the central portion of the visual field is achieved through habitually selecting out more peripheral portions. A narrowed and constricted centrality is then held to constitute the whole. The habit of favoring the *axis visualis* by eliminating a visual "residue" is, as we shall see, costly.

The third and last matter of *perspectiva* concerns what I call the "metaphysics of light." The Platonic equation *light = knowledge* comes through Augustine to emerge in Grosseteste's thought of the early thirteenth century. He writes in his *Commentary on the Posterior Analytics* that knowledge is a

> spiritual light which is shed upon intelligible things and the eye of the mind, and which has the same relation to the interior eye and to intelligible things as the corporeal sun has to the bodily eye and to visible things.[11]

Since knowledge is a seeing into the essence of things, a study of light reveals the transcendent plan behind the material universe. Light itself

is the first "form of corporeity," an embodiment of the primal impera-
tive, "Let there be light." Denser, more opaque bodies themselves represent more-distant emanations, being condensations of an energy
already dissipated. To be removed from light is to be cut off from the
source of knowing. It is to be cast into an abyss of ignorance, into which
is thrown all worthlessness. It is there the blind live. They and all darkened bodies are unable to turn toward the light source itself.

This then is *perspectiva*'s place by the fourteenth century, the
Quattrocentro. Between then and Shakespeare's Gloucester and Descartes's revenge of the early seventeenth century lies one important
development to which we now must turn. I mean the discovery of the
vanishing point of linear perspective.

3

The Vanishing Eye

5.633 . . . And nothing in *the visual field*
allows you to infer that it is seen by
an eye.
5.6331   For the form of the visual field is
surely not like this

Eye–

—Wittgenstein, *Tractatus*

The Vanishing Point of Sight

What if the eye's boundless ambition banished it beyond the infinite horizon? Would that event signal success or failure in the eyes of tradition? What if failure looks like success, and success failure? Herein lies Descartes's Promethean strategem, to disguise the worst as the best and let the gods choose accordingly. In one pile, Prometheus heaped the choicest cuts of the sacrificial bull and covered them with grizzle. In the other, the worst were covered with glistening fat. The gods could keep the portion they wanted. For a moment, they cannot decide. In the pause Descartes's opportunity knocks. His hope, like Prometheus's, is that discernment will not look below the surface and discover the reality of the bargain.

To illuminate vision's flight from time into an unimpeded, exertionless eternity, let me recount the story of Brunelleschi's demonstration of the vanishing point of linear perspective. This is the story of carrying a good thing too far and being carried away by it. The vanishing point was a new discovery but an old quest. It is that toward which the science of *perspectiva* had for centuries inclined—that toward which in pictorial space the eye is ineluctably drawn and from which all parallels

naturally radiate. It is the coincidence or perfect correspondence of artificial and natural space, the space of artist and the space of nature.

The vanishing point represents the virtual source and *telos* of the
visual field and lies a point beyond the field, in the invisible, the
unchanging, the empyreal. It draws sight to it, so to speak, from the
other side and thereby possesses a kind of angelic magnetism. It is what
we seem to look toward when regarding an unobstructed horizon with
100 percent visibility under excellent lighting. It is what, in not being
there, attracts presence and vision.

Brunelleschi's demonstration of its existence (in 1425 in the
Piazza del Duomo of Florence) is simple and ingenious. He had painted
a small panel in linear perspective to portray the baptistery that occupied a major portion of the square. He had his observers hold this close
to their faces and, through a hole drilled in it, look at a mirror reflection
of the painting. The location at which he stationed observers was the
same one from which he painted the scene. The visual accuracy of vanishing point perspective was then readily verified. A witness simply had
to compare the painting with the real thing right before his or her eyes.
Q.E.D.

The empirical conclusion of Brunelleschi's experiment in frontal
perspective establishes one thing. A carefully constructed, two-dimen-
sional representation of three-dimensional space can convincingly per-
suade the eye that illusion is reality. The construction, moreover, is
based on rigorous principles familiar to students of *perspectiva* and
employed by artistic precursors of Brunelleschi's discovery—for
instance, in Giotto. The principles of linear frontal perspective were
soon to be codified by Alberti, to whom we soon will turn. First, one
locates a centric point on the optical plane, the horizontal plane passing
through a viewer's eyes and containing the visual axis. The horizontal
plane extends infinitely in all directions around the viewer; directly in
front of the viewer, at the limit of vision, it forms the horizon. Then, one
determines where the artist as viewer is situated with respect to the
field. Using the artist's height (precisely, the distance from eye level to
the ground) as a measure, a series of orthogonals can be drawn conver-
gent to the centric point. The result is a kind of pyramidal grid that
stretches from a putative observer's eyes back into pictorial space to
where objects apparently vanish into the folds of visual distance. The
grid easily provides for the height of painted figures—building facades,
arches, viaducts, trellises, trees, human bodies. The technique brings to

the illusionist sense a strict mathematical control, thereby justifying the ways of deception to the student of *perspectiva*.

There was nothing geometrically new in the technique. Euclid had said that the size of a perceived object was a function of the visual angle, and the smaller the angle, the smaller the object. In fact, catoptrics, the optics of reflection, had spoken about matters relating to Brunelleschi's discovery. Flat-surfaced mirrors began to appear in thirteenth-century Europe, replacing the convex ones then in use. In catoptrics several theorems describe the *cathetus*, an extension of a line from the object to where it perpendicularly strikes the mirror surface. It is well proven that the distance an object appears to be *into* the virtual space behind the mirror is the same as its actual distance *from* the mirror's surface. With a flat mirror, the surface itself serves as the base of the visual cone. Taking into account this fact, Brunelleschi may have observed (as we can confirm) something striking by placing a mirror on the center of a wall of a perfectly quadrangular room and looking directly into it: all edges of floor and ceiling, as they recede from his eyes, converge to a point identical to one between his reflected eyes themselves. An astonishing conclusion at once arises. The visual cone has an invisible Siamese twin in the mirror's virtual space. The visual cone constructed from the observer's eyes as vertex and connected by the *axis visualis* to the mirror as base is joined foot to foot to a second, ghostly one. Sharing the same base, it recedes along the *cathetus* until it comes to a point correspondent to that of the visual cone's vertex (see fig. 2). This second point, the mirror's "inner eye," is none other than the vanishing point.

The geometric derivation of the vanishing point discloses its meaning. It is the gazing eye's double. It is a portrait of the gaze gazing at itself, to which the rest of pictorial space—the arbors and *puti*, the madonnas and thrones, the monuments and chalices—bear witness. The eye looks into the distance . . . for itself. Dimly, it records an absence: that it does not belong to the visible world. Dimly, it senses its banishment. It leaps into the beyond, not at a part of the picture but at a transcendental point. It looks there in need, in hope.

The gazing eye is magnetically attracted to the vanishing point. This Brunelleschi and others knew. The application of *perspectiva* to the visual arts was fueled by this force. The great frescoes and canvasses of the Italian Quattrocentro bear testimony to power of this force. Our museums and artbooks would be impoverished without it. Yet *why* is the eye drawn in this way? The answer has to do with the gaze, what it

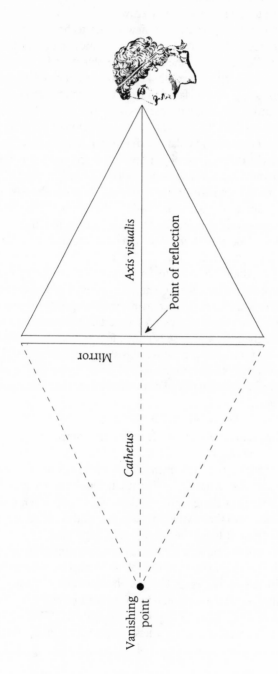

Figure 2. The geometry of Brunelleschi's vanishing point perspective. The hidden double of the gazing eye is the vanishing point.

defers, when it makes absent, and what in absentia it seeks. Like an angel looking for its earthly body, the gaze seeks out its embodied form. It feels deprived of its presence in the ongoing movement of life. It desires what it is not, yet senses dimly it is. It seeks union with its double in order that it might become itself.

The Window and the Veil

In 1435, over a century and a half before *King Lear*, Leon Battista Alberti wrote his *De pictura* (*Della pittura*, in the Italian edition.) The dedication is to Brunelleschi, and the effort is to codify and publicly present the results of vanishing point perspective. The work has a tripartite division. Book 1 has to do with the optics and geometrics of painting, book 2 with subject matter, and book 3 with the moral and intellectual preparation of the artist. Although our retrospective reading tends to cleave the mechanics of *perspectiva* from its ethical and aesthetic text, we need to be aware that such radical surgery leaves little else but a corpse for study.

Though relying on the science of optics, *De pictura* is written for painter and artisan. The terms of perspectival composition that Alberti offers differ little from what may be inferred from Brunelleschi. It is in his description of the process of composing a painting that we learn what perspective surreptitiously brings. "First of all," he tells us,

> on the surface on which I am going to paint, I draw a rectangle of whatever size I want, which I regard as an open window through which the subject to be painted is seen.[1]

Alberti writes more amply on the "open window." A painted picture was to be seen as

> transparent and like glass, that the visual pyramid passed right through it from a certain distance and with a certain position of the centric ray and of the light, established at appropriate points nearby in space. . . . Therefore a painting will be the intersection of a visual pyramid at a given distance, with a fixed center and certain position of lights, represented artistically with lines and colors of a given surface.[2]

What Alberti's thought most clearly reveals is where the artist's eye is located. One who gazes through an open window regards the scene to be painted, be it a landscape or a warm parlor room setting. The artist gazes from the outside in or the inside out. In either case, the artist's gaze comes from the other side of the frame. It is separated from what it beholds by something "transparent and like glass," yet harder and more impenetrable. That which holds the artist's viewing apart from the tableau, to form an "intersection" with the visual cone, is the imperviousness to the stop. It is that which abstracts the eyes from their organic milieu to render them more reliable, more celestial, more predictably geometric. It is that which removes sight from pulse and rhythm, tempo and time. It is that which blinds sight and causes Samson's agony. It is that with which Descartes forms his dark plot.

The interposition of a something, a frame, a window, between the eye and its field that removes the former from the latter is further depicted by Alberti's *velo,* or veil. The eye remains behind the veil, allowing the world to come in as if mapped in a configuration of spatial coordinates. The veil provides Alberti with a method of composition by making geometry visible:

> It is like this: a veil loosely woven of fine thread, dyed whatever color you please, divided up by thicker threads into as many parallel square sections as you like, and stretched on a frame. I set this up between the eye and the object to be represented, so that the visual pyramid passes through the loose weave of the veil.[3]

The artist then draws an evenly spaced grid on the surface to bear the composition and transfers contours, square by square, from object to surface. What is the veil? On one level, it is a device, a convenience that "affords the greatest assistance in executing your picture, since you can see any object that is round and in relief, represented on the flat surface of the veil."[4] At this level, the veil is usefulness itself, a systematic way of assigning to each point on an object a set of coordinates. Drawing the contents of a space belongs to the task of transcription, a reading off of numbers correlated with the grid. The veil is essentially a translation device. It facilitates accuracy in copying one spatial presentation to a second.

On another level, the veil as an article of dress is a way of hiding. What is hidden is the cost of the will's invention. One has eyes only for the benefits of a new system of copying. The *velo* works like a screen behind which the eye peeps out onto a field revealed to it. The veil provides safety and security. With thought occupied with the transposition of coordinates, attention is displaced from the confined and negated body of the copyist. While sight is dissipated toward the vanishing point, the geometric path made visible in its flight is faithfully recorded with the help of the veil. But no record is made of the space between veil and viewer or between viewer and drawing. That remains veiled. It is a concealed reality that remains concealed while attention is lavished on the illusionist creation. Lacking the stop, the copyist records the eternal objects stationed in the timeless field of vision.

The window and the veil. What Alberti enthusiastically describes—what Descartes with equal enthusiasm appropriates for his vindictive purpose—is the sense of sight engulfed by dreams of eternity. These two devices are ancillary to the vanishing point. Descartes seizes on the development. As long as the eye is oriented toward the vanishing point, the eye as incarnate vantage point vanishes from visual space. The vanishing point is the annunciation of the eye's vanishing. The vanishing point is the mirror image of the gazing eye, an absence that haunts the field and draws attention to it like a void. Henceforth, the eye will be as Wittgenstein draws it: apart from the empirical world, the world of perceptual experience. It has become a transcendental, a priori eye, the veritable model for Schopenhauer's metaphysical subject. The one who has eyes, the observer, will cease to see *through* his or her eyes to the field of objects, but will discount the eye as gatherer of vision. The eye will be the accident of personal viewpoint, the figment of subjectivity, the distortion of flesh, the red-rimmed and often teary eye. It will be vulgar. It will not be seen.

Window and veil further epitomize the transformation. The eye looks from behind a window, a gap in the wall, a slot that frames the visible world. For us to look in this fashion, the lighting must conform to specific conditions. Light must come from a source on the other side of the windowframe, either outside if looking out, or inside if looking in. If the lighting comes from a source on the same side as the observer, the effect is to dim the field. This is what happens upon turning on the cabin lights of a car while driving at night. Contours lose sharpness, spatial relations alter, depth of field is lost. When light is shed in the customarily darkened observer's side of the window, a new element appears. Like in the car for the one behind the wheel, so to with sight lit interiorly. The one who sees no longer sits invisibly gazing out, but participates bodily in the act of seeing. Sight no longer begins at a point just one point removed from its source, but includes the source itself.

The function of the window is to keep the eye on one side, the source of lighting on the other. The veil augments this function. It operates by making sure that vision will be one-way, *away from* the eye. Looking out from behind a veil, sight loses but little visual definition. But being looked at, the eye remains concealed. This is wonder of wonders! Any expression of its perception is thereby obscured, its knowledge blunted. It does nothing to reveal itself nor the one whose eye it is. It itself does not appear anywhere in the visible field of another person, yet it sees. Thus, while the eye is removed from the visible world, sight goes on—under the cover of invisibility. It need not worry itself about threat or attack, because it is not there at all. The veil provides the ultimate protection against insecurity. The veil is a refuge.

The veil also has a secondary function. It covers the vulgar, thereby keeping pure the vision of angel and God alike. The eye is of the body that breathes, pulses, and vibrates with manifestations of organic life. That life, more than anything else, is subject to time, change, and impermanence. The living eye that sees during life is the first organ to decay upon death. To close the lid of the eye then and acknowledge its final blinding is to greet this advent with modesty. Even during a lifetime, the eye is subject to the changes of illness, emotion, lighting conditions, wind, and weather. The eye brims with tears, dilates, goes wide with greed, narrows with wrath, swims with passion, burns with desire, is rheumy with a cold, discharges with conjunctivitis, and is bleary with lack of sleep. The physical eye is an amphitheater of suffering. It shows pain and vulnerability, partiality and constriction, fear and avoidance—hardly ways in which celestial beings manifest themselves. The more the displays are hidden from the angels, the stronger our belief that we are like them. And the more we will pretend to be like them.

Alberti's devices produced supremely well, far beyond his wildest dreams. The revolution wrought by linear perspective worked because of the great need it met. It sought to realize an idea Bacon expressed some three centuries early: "to make literal the spiritual sense." Literal-mindedness was to replace vague intuitions that indicated a higher reality. The window was literally open to eternity. The purpose of depicting the eternal was to justify an indifference to the temporal, the worldly, the mundane. God's geometrically ordered universe was an addition that was a subtraction. Take away the ephemeral—and, with it, feeling and sensation—and one gains entry into an unchanging divine cosmos. A perspectivally executed painting inculcated the feel of a reality acting behind and through the visible world. The orderly fashion with which the eye was magnetized and led to the vanishing point was proof of the hidden harmony. The fact that it was the eye's own love of concealment that drew its gaze into the depths of pictorial space—passing figures that diminished in size according to law—was lost in the exaltative mood. The engineering of a light-filled space that precisely mimicked that of nature was a triumph in need of celebration. It did not matter that it was an illusion. What mattered was that the illusion was properly evocative. What it evoked seemed to be a paradise regained.

A Digression on Leonardo

It would seem hasty after discussing two Florentine perspectivists of the Quattrocento not to include a third, especially since his fame overshadows theirs. I am thinking of Leonardo da Vinci, who belonged to the next generation after Alberti. Thoroughly conversant in optical theory, he made important contributions to visual anatomy, particularly with regard to the path of ocular light. He also harbored objections to Alberti's placement of the eye at a point outside the visual cone. This model, he argues, implies monocular vision (Brunelleschi placed a *single* hole for the eye in his historic panel), whereas actual vision is binocular. Such vision sees a curvature in "parallel" lines, thereby weakening the skeleton on which the illusion of perspective is hung.

But it is not Leonardo's contribution to *perspectiva* that now interests me. It is rather where he appears on the line extending between Alberti and Descartes. The first two are painters (Leonardo a great one, Alberti a minor one) who theorize about their work; the last, one who theorizes about the work of others, who theorizes with a vengeance. It is Leonardo who gives Descartes material for his plot. In a famous passage in the *Trattato della Pittura*, he writes:

> These [the scientific principles of motion, optics, mathematical laws, anatomy] are understood by the mind alone and entail no manual operation; and they constitute the science of painting which remains in the mind of its contemplators, and from it is then born the actual creation, which

is far superior in dignity to the contemplation or science
which precedes it.[5]

The Platonism of the thought is striking, and something like it must
have provided Descartes with the strategy he seeks. Leonardo argues
that the "science of painting" (= perspective) is intellectual even as its
product or application is manual. True, he values the result more than
the science, but he also requires the painter to foreknow or foresee the
outcome. To foresee is the primary application of the principles of
painting, the secondary application being the artwork itself. From this,
it is possible to follow the line of thought upon which Descartes seizes.
For it is the quality of intellectual vision (imagination) that gives life to
what is born on canvas. It is the mental seeing, when transferred by
craft and skill, to the flat surface that delights the eye in its fancy and
illusion. Though craft and skill transform the intellectual image to the
surface to yield an object "far superior in dignity" to that image, the
mental picture is nonetheless the source. It is where sight begins.

One can almost hear Descartes enumerating the insurmountable
difficulties he faces if he is to deprive sight of its fully embodied vision.
There is the vigilance of the faculty, how it keeps watch on any diminution of its intensity. There is its penetration, its ability to discern
essential natures. There is its self-reflexiveness, how vision participates
in a whole perception, of which it itself is a part—how vision sees itself.
And there is its availability to a reality encompassing it. At the heights
of his dilemma, enter Leonardo. What Leonardo's thought hints at is a
way around the last problem. If sight does not receive an impression of
what is outside it, if it simply portrays what lies inside, a mental image,
an imagined portrait, then perhaps the rest will fall into place.

Thus, Descartes.

> I have thus got back to where I wanted; I now know that
> even bodies are not really perceived by the senses or the
> imaginative faculty, but only by intellect; that they are per-
> ceived, not by being touched or seen, but by being under-
> stood.[6]

Descartes uses Leonardo's hint to his tactical advantage. The eye no
longer looks out from a window to take in the world in a single glance.
That setup is a trompe l'oeil that we have naively accepted. The world
is not the way it appears, nor is the eye so magnificently insightful. At

best, the sense of sight garners raw material for further processing by intellection. True sight (the revised account continues) looks in the reverse direction, *away* from the world. It looks toward Leonardo's "contemplation or science which precedes" the visual image. Here in the mind's eye are the preexisting forms of what exists in the field. Henceforth, the mind's eye becomes a faithful servant to sight, and the physical eye the vulgar counterpart.

Henceforth, the eye is no longer available to receive an impression of its place in an ordered cosmos, since it serves no cosmological end but a mental one.

Mister Molineux

Nearly two centuries after the revolutionary trump played out by the perspectivists, Descartes uses their ideology for his own subplot. Under the cloak of blindness, he sets out to emasculate the power of sight. He does this in such a persuasive way that almost four centuries later our sightedness has still not recovered. We see not with our eyes but with our brains. This is our Cartesian heritage. To set seeing equal to gazing is to alienate the eye from the field it illuminates and cleave it from an active receptivity that is its birthright. The eye becomes separated from the organic milieu, a mere observer, an instrument mechanically registering objects that reflect light back to it—an electronic eye. Its own light, the light of its perception, the light by which it can reveal itself as *in* (though not *of*) the field, is extinguished. Also extinguished is the coincidence of seer and seen, whereby the eye reveals its essential nature as self-seeing and self-knowing. The human eye becomes a mechanism of great pragmatic but limited ontological value. It can adequately be studied in corpses and animals; to wit, Descartes writing on the retinal image:

> having thus seen this picture in the eye of a dead animal,
> and having considered its causes, you cannot doubt that an
> entirely similar one is formed in the eye of a live man.[7]

The success of a revolution is measured by how fully it redefines the terms it inherits. After Descartes, questions of blindness preempt those of sightedness. Thinkers cease to be concerned with how the eye engenders perception of a field disclosed in revealing itself. They cease to study laws by which the eye grows perceptive after the blindness of imperception. Instead, the scope of inquiry shrinks. Thought becomes engrossed with problem of how someone with congenital blindness sees objects once sight is restored. Thinkers cease to think through the meaning of an awakened eye. Instead, they think about the particulars of a kind of vision assumed to be irreproachable.

A good example of the revolution's successful repositioning comes about fifty years after the *Dioptrics*, in 1693, when Locke receives a letter from his friend William Molyneux. A year later, in *An Essay Concerning Human Understanding*, Locke credits Molyneux with the following problem:

> Suppose a man born blind and now adult, and taught by his touch to distinguish between a cube and a sphere of the same metal, and nighly of the same bigness so as to tell when he felt one and the other, which is the cube and which the sphere. Suppose then the cube and sphere placed on a table and the blind man be made to see: *quaere*, whether by his sight before he touched them he could not distinguish and tell which is the globe, which the cube?[8]

Molyneux's problem deserves a moment's consideration.

In Molyneux's problem, the sort of repositioning I have in mind takes place. The question is no longer what sight adds to consciousness but what consciousness adds to sight. The consciousness that is an added-on, an appendix, is object recognition. The new problematic requires that we forego asking about the sea change that the blind man's consciousness undergoes. He who has lived a life without sight is to be queried about geometrical solids. We who forget how it is to move suddenly from darkness to a brightly lit room are his interrogators. We who forget forget the moment's stop, the shock of illumination that eradicates night and bright vision alike. Then, no objects narrow our attentiveness, which has expanded to meet the fact of being blinded. No habit of object identification survives in the intensity of not knowing where the world is. In that absence arises an exigence that interrogates us otherwise. "Who is that one who experiences the lostness?" That is the inquiry Descartes's ruse displaces.

Locke cites Molyneux's solution. Molyneux is quoted as saying:

Not. For though he has obtained the experience of how a globe, how a cube, affects his touch, yet he has not yet attained the experience that what affects his touch so or so must affect his sight so or so, or that a protuberant angle in the cube that pressed his hand unequally shall appear to his eye as it does in the cube.[9]

The point—with which Berkeley later agrees—is that the separate senses divide the world into separate realms. Each opens a different window to the world outside. The vista revealed to the one who gazes from the first window is wholly different from the tangibility felt by one probing from the second. There is no commonality, no commensurability. The specific kinds of sensory experience are not communicable, one to the other. They do not in and for themselves relate. This is a startling admission. It is a confession that the one who looks with eyes is not the same one who touches with hands. It attests to the lack of a unifying awareness, a *sensus communis*, able to receive impressions through different channels. The absence furthers the machinations of Descartes. It guarantees that sight and touch, hearing and smell and taste, no longer speak a common language, no matter what dialects they use. They do not understand one another. They do not look from one place into one and the same world. They cease to disclose facts about themselves or one another. They no longer register a failing acuity in a sister sense.

Loss of the mother tongue in sensory experience is overlooked in a growing preoccupation with object consciousness. The capability requires a highly selective focus, multiple discriminations, and a power to keep things separate from one another. In the service of such attentiveness, sight is almost overwhelmed by diversity in the visual field. Its constant need is to differentiate and to order one thing after another. Differential sightedness reveals the manifold of the world, yet is inglorious. A search for differentia—the criteria of identification and reidentification—belies a way of looking away. The one who makes distinctions lacks all distinctions. That one has grown invisible.

Without the mother tongue of organic experience, sight retreats from contact with sensory channels that hold disagreement with its findings. From its place of hiding, to multiply things seems natural rather than a displacement from the primal question. From its hiding, to spare Occam's razor is to spare the user unwanted pain. The lover of multiples does not want to understand the underlying issue, namely, from what awareness does the object world spring?

The source of objectification is not at its mouth. It is that to which Descartes's genius for revenge blinds sight. We come back to the stop. When the habits of listing, sorting, weighing, and arranging the furniture of the world are momentarily arrested, the awareness undergoes a slight shift. The restlessness of conducting an inventory gives way to an inner composure. One ceases to be a manager of things—a something among other somethings—and instead takes one's place as an inhabitant of a cosmos. The return is to an original position of embodied awareness and its native perceptivity. It is this—Samson's discovery—that the stop brings.

The same movement toward origin causes a radical change in the relation among the specific senses. The frozen time of enumeration and identification of objects burdens sensory experience with linearity. Perception must occupy only one sense at a time. Immediacy is inadequate to the task of translating the language of one sense into that of another. We must turn to comparative judgment, measuring, say, the visual shape of a cube with what memory holds as its tactile feel. Different channels of sense experience do not occupy the same moment until a selective attention is arrested. The specific experiences of different senses present themselves as aspects of a single impression, textured according to diverging sensory inputs. The various senses are no longer untranslatable, one to the other, since the key has been provided. But neither are they interchangeable, as if each has no mark of distinction. One can see with the hands and touch with the eyes, but then it is still the hands seeing and the eyes touching.

The problematic of Molyneux's problem arises from the frozen frame of its projection. But then, the stroboscopic snapshot is Descartes's replacement for the continuous movie reel. Sight has been infected with the gaze, and now the gaze contaminates all senses. Other senses must be measured against sight and found incommensurately wanting. But put an end to the timeless state. Start the action again, and the convergence appears whereby different sensory channels point to an underlying unity of sensory experience. That unity is Samson's way.

Part
Two

WHAT THE
BLIND SEE

We must therefore break away once and for
all from the metaphors which depict
consciousness as a luminous circle round
which there is nothing to its own eyes but
darkness. On the contrary, the shadow is at
the center.
—Gabriel Marcel

4

Blindness and the Sign

Blindness and Compensation

Blinding is a punishment, *the* archaic form of punishment. Blinding deliberately inflicts pain of darkness. Darkness is absence of meaning, an absence difficult to bear. To be cast into a self-enveloping darkness is to be thrown back onto primordial terror. Order—represented by the visual field—is suspended. The hounds of chaos are thereby set loose to devour articulated space and the frame of objects. Where things are stripped of name and form, how can we keep our bearings? How can we avoid being paralyzed by fear of movement and risk of collision? The dark is a screen on which fear, of the known and the unknown, is projected.

The *arche*-punishment is the most consuming, the most totalizing. It is what enslaves most deeply while still stopping short of complete brutalization. Thus, in a sense it represents the most *human* of punishments, inasmuch as it—unlike mutilation, gladiatorial combat, jailing, forced labor, or even psychological rehabilitation—leaves intact a potentiality of being. In this guise, death as punishment is no punishment at all, but a foreshortening of pain, conflict, and contradiction in one blow. Blindness, furthermore, is a most human form of punishment because it arises from the most human of motives: revenge. Nietzsche has detailed the involutions of a primal compensatory justice that lies at the heart of social learning. Paying one's enemy back by striking out his or her eyes satisfies the felt debt and leaves the other in a state of servitude. In a state of servitude, yet still deeply human, for, as I said, like evokes like. The motive behind blinding evokes the same in the blinded. At least, this is Gloucester's moment of truth. Just prior to being blinded by Regan's vengeful hand, he prophesies, saying: "I shall see/The winged vengeance overtake such children" (*King Lear* III. vii).

One act of revenge exchanged for another. Murder of the Philistine host in exchange for Samson's blinding. The formulation makes it
seem like an ironclad exchange system. There are occasions, however,
when a different compensation comes into being. Then the spirit of
revenge does not inevitably recur. With the other compensation comes
a deeper, though still human, perception. I am thinking of a mode I
alluded to earlier. It is poised perception, a gathering unto a moment of
novelty. It is perception of tracings of hidden meaning. It is the perception that belongs to the stop.

When we look toward myth for clues to a docile form of compensation, the figure of Teiresias is striking. Teiresias, a Phoenician (that is,
a foreigner), was punished with blindness, although accounts differ as
to why. Some say he inadvertently came upon Athena at her bath and
she blinded him. Others say that Aphrodite acted when he passed her
over in a beauty contest. Still others say it was Hera and because he had
settled a dispute she had with Zeus in Zeus's favor. All accounts agree
that pain of darkness was inflicted as payment for a wrong Teiresias
knowingly or unknowingly committed. All accounts, furthermore,
agree that the perpetrator repented of the act or that a good Samaritan
saw the injustice of Teiresias's blindness. According to law, however, a
punishment once administered cannot be completely undone. Pain
inflicted cannot be erased; penalty exacted cannot be reversed. Only a
modification is permissible, and a compensation returned to the suf-
ferer. How much modification modifies punishment depends on how
successfully one mimics the other, that is, how well the compensation
mimics what the punishment takes away. In the case of Persephone,
whose punishment was exile in Hades, compensation was freedom in
strict proportion to how much food she had consumed in exile. The
folktale of Sleeping Beauty is clearer. After black magic sentences the
heroine to death, the only clemency lies in modifying the terms of punishment to a hundred-year sleep. Her compensation is life, albeit a life
of nonexistence.

If we look at Teiresias, the law of compensation is operative. Teiresias loses his eyesight to vengeance. He is thereafter confined to his
body, his organic shell. He must grope his way without the effortless
outreach of vision. That horizon will not open to receive him. His
present whereabouts cannot be gleaned from a few easy hints in the
visual field. He must find himself, if he is able to, within an opaque interior, with its unknown mode of access to objects. He must, if he can,
learn a new language, of sensation, with which to speak and be spoken

to by his experience. None of the radical alteration—obscuration and a colorless world—can be undone. Teiresias seems already a Samson, ready to grind down the order that punished him. But this is not the case. For the blindness he is given mythological compensation that dissolves the potential for a repetition of revenge. What is the gift? That of reading signs, with special emphasis on second sight, prophecy, or divination.

Divinatory Perception

That the blind can read signs and possess (or are possessed by) second sight is ancient tradition. That their deficiency in sight is compensated for by ordination of other perceptual powers belongs to the same tradition. Tradition also has it that Teiresias was the greatest of blind soothsayers of his time, and one among many. The account has it that Athena was moved to pity after striking him blind and said, "Open Teiresias's ears that he might understand the language of prophetic birds."

We must not, however, think that such powers belong exclusively to the blind. Might the ability also arise by birth or practice? In both cases, to be able to read signs, perception must pass from its closed circle to the open pathway, from objectification to a frontier along which the concealed emerges from the unconcealed, the about-to-be-manifest from the manifest, and in which the second divulges the secret of the first. Only when the transition is accomplished is an avenging impulse drained of its maleficent power.

What is the nature of passage from object identification to sign reading? We have to retrace the steps in reverse of Descartes's dark plot against tradition. For traditional perception, the world presents itself through signs by which to divine meanings of things and thus know what action is required of the reader. Reading skill is distributed along a hierarchy of talent, inherited or acquired by elite training. Being hierarchical, it supports an established and exclusionary order. Those who are illiterate, who cannot read signs, are excluded. It is thoroughly anti-democratic and opposed to the political sentiments of Descartes. His new order will overthrow the divinatory sign in order to install another token bearing the same title, "sign," in a position of supreme power. Thus revised and revisionary, a sign, stripped of its revelatory power, will henceforth take its place as a mere representative of the light—not of the light itself. It will be egalitarian because citizens will be able to read it without elite training or rare, inherited talent. Meaning will thereby be bent to serve rather than thwart a democratic impulse.

What received understanding is Descartes compelled to react against? It is one in which nature speaks, and humankind responds, perceptually. Writing a century before Descartes's *Dioptrics*, Paracelsus immerses himself in a study of divinatory perception. He says:

> It is not God's will that what he creates for man's benefit and what he has given us should remain hidden. . . . And even though he has hidden certain things, he has allowed nothing to remain without exterior and visible signs in the form of special marks—just as a man who has buried a hoard of treasure marks the spot that he may find it again.[1]
> (p. 120)

Divinatory perception passes through a surface of things marked with signs to indicate veins of deeper meaning. It passes along the pathway by means of similarity and analogy—by means of the imagination—to reach an as-yet-uncovered truth. A surface mark is not essentially self-referential, as referring wholly to a closed system of signs established by convention and making reference only to other signs, never to things. Such a view devitalizes the sign and makes it a mere mark on the paper—more of Descartes's diabolical work. The philosophical motif of constituting a sign through a mental activity erases tracings of hidden meaning. Its appeal is to self-will: Is not the sign a human invention? Its inventiveness is to consume the attention in classification and representation—a mental construction of the sign—and to leave nothing to return to a search for signification in the world. Inquiry becomes ingrown, reflecting more and more of itself.

It is otherwise with divinatory perception. The sign is not a cipher arbitrarily assigned to denote one thing among many things, but a secret aspect of the thing itself. Text and world are magically held together, intermingled by force of sympathy into one efficacious whole. A sign is not a repetition or redundancy of the thing denoted, requiring only dictionary or encyclopedia to solve the unknown and add it to the store of knowledge. A sign is secrecy itself that invites risk of discovery by dint of perception. It is mask, disguise, camouflage, cloak, dissembling. It is intention both to appear as other than it is and to reveal a way into the maze. Once uncovered by retracing a pathway of discovery, the sign connects the invisible with the exterior and visible. Its essential reference is to an interior world, the world where light is shrouded, occluded, or absent. Its reference is to mystery.

Such knowledge involves interpretation. More precisely, it coincides with interpretation. To know is to pass from the exterior mark beneath to what is meant by it. Meaning lies dormant, like unspoken thought, within the heart of things until interpretation unlocks it. *To interpret,* in its root sense, is to negotiate an exchange; *pretium* is the price. Interpreting is mediating between two unlikes: the one who holds the goods and the one who wants them. For an exchange to take place, interpretation must perceive likeness and correspondence. Under the aegis of the go-between, the thing that asks that its meaning be taken surrenders it to the thing asking for that meaning. The outer sign thereby becomes emblazoned with inner signification. The inner sign, conversely, submits itself to the tracing of an outer utility.

Paracelsus notices:

> we men discover all that is hidden in the mountains by signs and outward correspondences; and it is thus that we find out all the properties of herbs and all that is in stones. There is nothing in the depths of the seas, nothing in the heights of the firmament that man is not capable of discovering. There is no mountain so vast that it can hide from the gaze of man what is within it; it is revealed to him by corresponding signs. (pp. 120–21)

This exercise of intelligence opens a text of being and engages it. It is hermeneutic and semiotic. It is hermeneutic because it allows signs to speak for themselves and interpretatively listens to their inner resonances. It is semiotic because it defines and locates signs and because it studies their interconnection—because it assembles a syntax of signs. A search for a buried likeness whose trace lies on the surface of things has different forms. In the human sciences and medicine in particular it issues in the doctrine of signatures that deciphers special marks of health and disease. The doctrine applies the law of similiars to plant and animal kingdoms. For instance, nightshade (*Belladonna*) is indicated for fever because its fruit mimics the fire-red complexion of a febrile patient. Poison oak (*Rhus*) is appropriate for joint ailments because its vine copies the gnarled appearance of arthritic tissue. Signatures, moreover, are sometimes written one over the other and can only be interpretatively disentangled. Take chicory (*Chichorium*), known for its beneficent effects with respect to eye disease because its blossom is sky-blue and seeks the sun. One can infer a further resemblance that helps decode its precise meaning in the pharmacopeia. Paracelsus writes:

> The chicory stands under a special influence of the sun; this is seen in its leaves, which always bend toward the sun as though they wanted to show it gratitude. Hence it is most effective while the sun is shining, while the sun is in the sky. As soon as the sun sets, the power of chicory dwindles. (p. 123)

The doctrine of signatures exhibits the general features of reading signs. Outward manifestations are beacons of a light that has eternally shone through things themselves from an intelligence beyond. That light is constant while awaiting another intelligence someday to perceive the veiled similarity and recognize that fruit and flower mirror secret properties implanted there since beginningless time.

The doctrine of signatures is a synchronic application of divinatory perception. Secrets of nature hide, but "there is nothing that nature has not signed in such a way that man may discover its essence" (p. 121). What is more hidden than the future? To apply the perception diachronically is to divine the yet-to-be from indications present to hand. Such perception gleans from among immediate clues of an emerging order of events. The new order has been inscribed in things since creation. Paracelsus: "Nature is the sculptor: she endows everything with the form which is also the essence, and thus the form reveals the essence" (p. 121). The essence of a stately oak is written in the form of an acorn, or the mature human in the form of a germ cell. Divinatory perception is able to open the book of knowledge—which houses a truth in relative immunity to change—and to read the meaning of *this* time as well as time to come. Signs are legible because language is entrusted with such purpose and has faithfully and persistently carried out its task.

Therein lies the crux of the matter. To perceive divinatorily is to read. That which is written, moreover, is in a language imbued with a life and force that ours, *this* language I write in, lacks. That force is a visionary one. A language of signs, that which Teiresias listens to and Paracelsus studies, emits a light that permits detection of hidden meaning. It lets itself be seen. Such a language differs radically from one I currently employ. The first dwells as a power among things, perhaps as *the* primary power by which things are enabled to disclose themselves. It belongs to things, is part of the community of things, and is forever engaged in unveiling the essence of things whose place it shares. It differs in one fundamental respect from the language I use. The difference throws a cloak of invisibility over the first language. It has not yet been blinded by revenge.

Yet there is a reticence to the sign even before Descartes's irreversible act. The sign is veiled, does not wear its meaning on its sleeve, and is not understood until drawn into the open. What is this natural reticence in language? I should say, languages, because the same holds true also for painting, dance, music, mime, and architecture, in addition to verbal language. Meaning must be let to appear. Relation—between the sign and what it signifies, between nightshade and its curative properties with respect to fever—must be allowed to show itself. Meaning resides in an indissolvable triad. So residing, it is perpetually at risk of falling back into obscurity. There is the inner virtue marked by an outer tracing and there is that which likens one to the other. Perception of the luminous link breaks down when a single element is not gleaned—when mark is not noticed, inner property (though suspected) is not discerned, or each is noted but without connection.

The triadic analysis of meaning significantly modifies one that Peirce offers. In his theory of triadic relations, a sign (or "representamen," as he calls it) is that which is intended to mean by an irrefragible unity of signification. It "stands to somebody for something in some respect of capacity" (p.99).[2] What I have called a "sign"—the first of three elements constituting the triad—Peirce terms the "interpretant," a mental reproduction of the sign itself. The second element is that which is signified, or (for Peirce) the object. The third or relating element Peirce calls the "ground," that which is similar between interpretant and object. The primary focus of Peirce's analysis is the conventional sign, visible aspect of a mental construct that is so instrumental in perceptual reconstruction of the world. He admits that a sign "is a Representamen with a mental Interpretant" (p. 100). Nonetheless, he allows provision for signs that inhabit the realm of things and on occasion show themselves to a human mind. In his preference to call them "Representamens," he acknowledges that

> if a sunflower, in turning toward the sun, becomes by that
> very act fully capable, without further condition, of repro-
> ducing a sunflower which turns in precisely corresponding

ways toward the sun, and of doing so with the same repro-
ductive power, the sunflower would become a Representamen of the sun. (p. 100)

We can, furthermore, say the language differs from our own in
another crucial way. Though divinatory perception can be recorded, no
record guarantees fidelity. What is perceived—a triadic meaning that
dwells as a force among things—is especially susceptible to decay and
distortion. The emitted light is highly perishable. Various compendia of
Paracelsus and other workers represent experiments in perserving an
unstable immediacy. The resulting concoction offers proof of a very limited success. Their books read as a hodgepodge of magic, theurgy,
astrological observations, botanical and zoological facts, hermetic for-
mulas, and folk wisdom. They underline the great problem for a language of signs: intersubjectivity. If it were said that divinatory perception is essentially incommunicative, the disclaimer would not be far
from true.

Preservation is unproblematic for the language I currently employ. Hence, neither is communicability. Meaning is a binary affair
between the sign that signifies and what is signified. The third term,
their relation, has been exorcised, or rather bled to insubstantiality.
That is fortunate since the problem of perishability is also eradicated.
Sign and signified partake in a single function, which is to refer to one
another. The word *cat* makes reference to an idea of the feline creature
denoted by the sign, while that notion in turn refers back to the sign
and the frame of other signs in which it is situated. Both sign and signified share a kinship. Both are signs. Their association depends on a
system of such binaries, welded into a whole, mutually supporting one
another, and making travel without breaks possible throughout the system. Thus, the dictionary or encyclopedia that perserves and communicates meaning at one blow.

It is extraneous to the inquiry how the signified sign "fits" in with
things. A picture of language and things that share a common dwelling
place and purpose has been lost. The former no longer works to reveal
the meaning of the latter, in concentric circles of ever-widening meaningfulness, until the meaning of humanity's place in the cosmos is
encompasssed. Instead, things have been pushed to just beyond the
surface of perception and knowledge, to form a swirling, undifferentiated sea that shapes sign and signified alike but does not partake of
meaning per se. They are not needed because the text itself supplies the

light of meaning. In fact, the text composed wholly of verbal signs supplies a glaring light, so glaring that it blinds the reader to the world.

From where does the blinding light arise? We should not be surprised at this turn of Descartes's vengeance. Listen:

> If the understanding intends to examine something that can be referred to [the concept of] body, then we must form in the imagination as distinct an idea of this thing as we can; and in order to provide this in a more advantageous way, the actual object represented by this idea must be presented to the external senses.[3]

Questions as to the origin of signs replace those of the origin of luminosity. Theories of natural signs (the smile as natural sign for joy) or of a "sympathy" of a sign for brute reality come into being. But something is changed. The blinded language forgets, like the blind man, what colors and visual shapes look like, forgets the revelation of meaning that pulses from the heart of the things themselves.

Descartes's Omen

Although Descartes's motives are contradictory, he is not aware of this. Unawares, he is able to put on the mantle of blindness to seek revenge against the sighted. Perception, he assumes, will be taken from its traditional haunts—the angelic realms of Plato—and returned to its rightful habitat, and the world let in through the organism's sensitivity. Descartes's genuis is this: an idea of vision designed to blind the eye's capability to receive a revitalizing energy of higher intelligence. Eye becomes lens or window whose curvature is a passive receptivity. Revenge is what he seeks, because he is orphaned child who feels a tradition of sightedness has stolen his patrimony and left him blind. He is the democrat who, below the walls of oligarchy, plans his assault on the citadel.

The plan has multiple foci as part of a diversionary strategy. One is directed against a language sanctioned by traditon. We can imagine him to reason thus: The sign is a natural ally of the eye. Eye is to read, the sign and sign is to be read by the eye. Does not the sign harbor its secret luminousness, just as the eye harbors its secret receptivity that is ready to be illuminated as soon as the eyelid rises? Does not the sign divulge what hides beneath its surface just as the eye burrows through the visual field, discovering concealed objects? Hence, for a plot of vengeance to be effective, blinding must be extended to language.

There is little doubt that Descartes operated on some such presumption. An overzealous democrat, he fails to see that a luminous language supports the perception of the blind. He blinds the eye in order to restore knowledge to her throne through proprioceptive vision. Reawakening an effortful perception proper to the organism, he hopes to rediscover the way to Dover. Language too will be blinded. Blinded language—signs that appear effortlessly—absolve the perceiver of effort. Blinded language, therefore, works against his duplicitous plotting. In his headlong rush to wield the cane, Descartes looks to see whether language hinders or helps the disembodiment of sight. By the time he pauses, it is too late.

Like a procrastinating Hamlet, Decartes turns from the omen he receives. Like Hamlet, unable to acknowledge a responsibility it awakens, he tries to blunt his perception by discrediting its source. This too is intellectualization of revenge. In any event, it is undeniable that Descartes knows how traditional language speaks, because he has been spoken to. Descartes receives a sign.

On the night of 10 November 1619, Descartes dreams three dreams. That he recognizes their intimate form of address is corroborated by the fact that they reveal to him his vocation as a philosopher, a Samson, and a destroyer of tradition. The dreams are seen as signs. I present them as recorded by Descartes's biographer Baillet. In the first, Descartes is driven by an "impetuous wind, which, carrying him away in a kind of vortex, made him spin three or four times on the left foot."[4] He seeks shelter in a college church but passersby distract him and he awakens. He immediately understands the dream language and interprets it as a reproach for his sins. He then falls asleep again, dreams of the "goods and evils" of his life, and is awakened by a thunderclap.

In the third dream, Descartes finds two books on his desk, a dictionary and a *Corpus omnium veterum poetarum Latinorum*. He opens the second to the line *Quod vitae sectabor iter*, "What way in life should I follow?" from a poem of Ausonius.[5] There is a stranger who appears, reciting a line that begins *"Est et non."* Descartes, unable to find the poem in the anthology, cites another beginning with the same line, but meets with the same lack of success in the book. The stranger disappears. Descartes then *dreams* an interpretation of this dream: "that the *Dictionary* wanted to say [nothing other than] all the sciences collected together;

and that the [collection of poems] . . . showed in particular and in a more particular manner Philosophy and Wisdom conjoined." Descartes then reflects on the contrast of poetry and philosophy, in that former is often more "serious" and "sensitive" than the latter. Philosophy has only reason to support it, while poetry is filled with "the divinity of enthusiasm" and the "power of the imagination."[6]

Descartes's dream within a dream continues. The inner dream dreams of interpreting the outer dream. That is, Descartes dreams that he dreams in the language of signs and begins to read. The inner dream continues, according to Baillet's transcript, as follows:

> By the poets assembled in the *Anthology* he understood revelation and the enthusiasm that, he made bold to hope, would continue to single him out. The piece "*Est et non*," which is the *Yes and no* of Pythagoras, he understood to be the truth and falsity in all human knowledge and the profane sciences.[7]

Then the shells of the dreams, inner and outer, rupture and Descartes is awake. He remembers the form of the dream's address and the interpretative response it provoked. He remembers what signs were, how they were detected, and how he unlocked their secret meanings. The process of disclosure is so transparent to him that

> seeing that all these things worked out so well with his inclinations, he was bold enough to convince himself that it was the Spirit of Truth that had wanted to open to him the treasures of all the sciences in this dream.[8]

With this pronouncement, Descartes's moves into contradiction. He dreams in a language that he interprets through a second-level dream. Dream and interpretation resonate with meaningfulness throughout his waking life. Yet the means to actualize their hidden import is denial. Revenge denies the sign's concealed message and robs it of its place among the things of life. The dregs of devitalized language that remain are incapable of furthering Descartes's ulterior aim of letting the blind see. He is left with a broken circle whose ends seek vainly for closure of purpose. Like Hamlet, his final act is one of destroying the self to save the self.

Signs that do not see and cannot be seen by eyes that are blind. A dream of great auspiciousness yields a ransom of pain. Was the dream out of its time or the time inhospitable to the dream? How did interpretation err? We must no longer avoid searching for the antidote to the modern age's dispiriting impulse that still speaks to itself in the heart of language.

The Milieu of Descartes's Reading

Descartes dreams of an opening to a forgotten poem, *Est et non*. He then dreams an interpretation of it, that it refers to the truth values of Pythagoras, thought's agreement with what is. He awakens and accepts dream and interpretation, sign and reading dreamt of that sign. Reading determines a line of action. The line, which I have studied in detail, curves back on itself in self-defeat. How are we to understand the curvature of failure? How has the sign failed to uncover an act that corresponds with it?

Meaning shows itself through the triad nature of sign, signified, and relation. Yet certain boundary conditions must be rigorously enforced. These pertain to the state of receptivity, or, as Peirce would say, the quality of the interpretant. Perceiver must correspond with sign or become a medium through which sign manifests. A state of preoccupation renders one unavailable to an appearance of the sign. The sign itself is not taken in, only a distorted rendition of it. One needs only to examine Descartes's testimony to understand how these conditions fail to obtain. The relation (or ground, in Peirce's terminology) through which meaning appears has not been prepared—a task that has no great appeal for Descartes. He acknowledges that preparation provides an uncluttered space in which the sign's intelligibility can be writ. It makes provision for, as he notes in the *Regulae*, "a conception, formed by unclouded mental attention, so easy and distinct as to leave no room for doubt in regard to the thing we are understanding."[9] Such a "conception formed by an unclouded and attentive mind, one that originates solely from the light of reason" stands for its similar, the actual sign.[10] But when it comes to preparing the ground, Descartes remains passive, mesmerized by the thought of an achievement—an avenging—and unmindful of the law of process. He wishes for a result, forgetful of the effort needed. He forgets the stop.

His lack of interest indicates a concealment. When Descartes juxtaposes sign and reading, there is hidden agenda. His is to ascertain whether all has "worked out so well with his inclinations"—that is, his plot to overthrow tradition. But this is a poor measure of soundness. A reading through it determines no more than its acceptability to the ego. The depths of interpretation are drastically foreshortened. Descartes settles for a lesser that is a greater only in terms of his backward-looking motive. The sign falls on eyes blinded by ambition. He cannot read because he cannot see. The reading is misread.

Descartes fails to prepare for a relation that brings meaning to light. The fact does not detract from his conviction vis-à-vis his reading. But where the question "Convinced by what?" is ignored, great danger arises of a self-serving disclosure. No further opportunity for commentary, revision, self-interrogation, or critique is seized. This is the case with the Cartesian moment at the beginning of modern thought. No room is left for an alternative interpretation of the opening line of the dream-poem *Est et non*. Descartes's ego, the seat of intellect, is in charge. The chief proclivity of modern thought, thereby set in motion, has not yet come to rest.

Had Descartes been able to pause, another reading would have presented itself. In the alternative, the highlighted line speaks of the affirmation and denial of existence itself, the *Sum* or "I am" that forms the cornerstone of Descartes's thought. That one's existence, in its entirety and in each and every aspect, is subject to these contradictory forces is the crux of the dream-sign. At each moment, the *yes* and the *no* are conjoined, each striving for dominance, neither yielding ground. One is in agreement with what is taking place, the other is in disagreement. In addition, the line refers specifically to the conjunction, the *et*. The conjunction itself differs in form and energy from either force. *Et* signifies an invisible third factor, a new force of reconciliation. The presence of the reconciling factor provides a conduit of novelty to the situation. Inner change through growth becomes possible. Its origin lies in a new dimension, higher than that of affirmation or denial. But its point of application should be familiar. It is the stop.

5

The Organism of Text

Prefatory to Reading

What do the blind know of divinatory perception? When their loss of sight is compensated for, what are they given? First and foremost, the stop. With the stop, the wheel of repetition, the samsaric retribution of an eye for an eye, a tooth for a tooth, is momentarily brought to an end. They are no longer impelled by a revenge that devours each present to appease an insatiable appetite for pain. Thought's vindictiveness is to capture the attention: they, the blind, are no longer prey to that. They no longer are slaves to repetitive obsession since they cease plotting to repay their perpetrators with like kind. Freed by the stop from the law of distraction, they then gain a concentration and awareness of what the world says and how things speak. They gain an ableness. That is the first and lesser gift of the stop.

The stop stops a continuous, automatic leave-taking of percipient energy. Such energy is automatically and without effort drawn into a conceptual frame that moment-by-moment contructs the world. It empowers the frame, thereby losing its own identity, power, and sense of origin. Energy mistakes the form given it by the frame for itself, for perception itself. It thereby finds itself separate from the world. Separate, it conceives its task as a detached onlooker to an activity of which it is not a part. It grows forgetful of how it bears witness to its own cocreation.

The stop stops percipient energy from animating the conceptual frame. Energy that no longer magnetizes ideas and concepts remains in its organic habitat. Such energy, by virtue of the stop, no longer escapes the fleshy folds of the body. Instead, it energizes a network of relations constituting the organism, thereby resensitizing the milieu and awakening a responsiveness uniquely nonmental. "Body" ceases to be an idea within the frame of ideas, implying other ideas such as "extension" and "motion." It becomes instead a container of an unknown identity through which move currents of sensation, themselves percipient and mindful of a reality to which the organism belongs. One's body becomes available to an attentiveness of an entirely different order.

The body of sensitivity, available to a higher awareness, is, for the blind, not a state but an episode. It belongs to the moment. It arises in the moment of the stop, flourishes while the stop vibrates throughout the organism, and perishes even as the last echoes of the stop can be heard. It has no permanence and must be regained, if at all, by dint of effort. The second and greater gift of blindness is not the stop, but the effort to return to the stop. By a kind of exertion quite different from that of the sighted in their application of the conceptual frame, the blind can repeat the action of the stop. The action ceases to allow percipient energy through the act of intellectual apprehension to construct a world, and maintains that energy within the organism. It is the act of self-containment. By the act, the blind repeat the stop.

The stop returns the blind to the body, the language of sensitivity, and the effort to abide therewith—in the reverse order. Body and language, organism and text, both take their existence from persistence of effort, that is, from a unique exertion having to do with a direction of perception. More precisely, both body and language, from the standpoint of perception, are results of the peculiar brand of effort. They become manifest at the end phases of a sufficiently deepened effort. Their absence does not invalidate a particular effort on the part of the blind. They know much groping is more important than a little success. Absence of results indicates that a certain threshold has not yet been reached. Effort provides a means whereby language gets instated. A sensitivity develops to events quite apart from their mental constructs. The language tells things about the perceiver's state, about resistance, blockage, receptivity, relation, and openness. The form of the instated language is the milieu through which such facts are expressed. It is the body.

In the expression *the language of the body,* the *of* is not the possessive but the relational. The body does not have its language, but through its language it *is,* that is, is allowed to stand forth as itself. The body exists as a vitality or vital force through sensation, its vocabulary. The language of the body is a language of presence. The text of presence is that of someone being present within the habitat of the body. It is a text of preparing for such a presence, of working to maintain presence, and of being without it after it departs. That someone is present is experienced as a *who*. The one present, in this case, is an unknown identity. Whenever it truly takes a name, it is called "myself," "I."

The stop is a vehicle for reengendering the body. It is a secret seed given to the blind as recompense for their deprivation of sight. It opens up to a secret text whose language becomes legible once the stop is cultivated. The secret of the text is its nearness to things, its lack of distance, its inseparability, its love of the world. It is easily miscible with what there is. Though the text is not to be read by the eyes, it is not not to be read. The eyes of the sighted are a hindrance to reading only so long as they remain oblivious to the stop. The eyes of the sighted cannot read as long as they express desire for the effortless and angelic. Once the rutted path the blind know is walked, the stop yields its treasure to any who follow it.

The stop is the protoeffort. All effort is directed, implicitly or explicitly, toward cessation of thought construction. This is implied by the change of direction induced by the stop, from exiting to reentering. Identification of the stop with an initial act of will belongs to ancient tradition. It is said in Samkhya philosophy that *mano niroddyavya*, the mind must be arrested, or again, in the *Katha Upanisad*, "That they call the supreme goal, when the five perceptions conjointly with the mind (*manas*) come to a standstill and intellect (*buddhi*) makes no motion." It would be misleading, however, to speak of stopping thought as the aim of the stop or as the effect of the initiation of will. The stop takes place, and, as a result, thought stops. The aim of the stop is different. It is to remember the twofoldness of human life.

Human life is dual in that, from a single vantage point, perception looks in two directions. Perception looks at functional life, self-will, thought, and desire. There it perceives its state—of wanting, judging, comparing, feeling, or sensing. Perception of function forms the basis of reflection or action. Perception also looks at energy life, the movement of energy prior to the forms of functionality. This is the Life of our life, that which is a source for particular undertakings of functional life. Perception thus takes note of how percipient energy enters life on our ordinary level, how it animates forms of life, and how it remains distinct from these forms. Where the duality or double perception is lost, so is the stop. Conversely, where the stop is practiced, the twofold perception is restored.

When the blind are compensated for their debility, they are given the stop. What they are therewith granted is probably worth more than their loss. They are given to perceive through twofoldness. Their per-

ception opens not only to functional life (minus sightedness), but also
to the energy that animates that state. They perceive the manifest and
that from which the manifest arises. They look into not only human
nature but also that from which human nature springs. It is small wonder that we call their gift "divination."

What the Stop Stops

The stop is the protoeffort. All exertion toward perception repeats the
stop. Repetition is required because of flux of the milieu. That which is
attained is of the moment and unless renewed stands at risk of reversal,
annulment, depletion, or disappearance. Permanence is a category by
which the mind interprets the organic text; Kant writes "synthesizes,"
but that misunderstands how sensation is a well-unified event. The idea
that an achievement is once and for all is an intellectualization. It
encapsulates a perception that looks only one way, toward functional
life. A twofold perception takes into account the movement of percipient energy from which specific forms of perception spring. That flux is
constant, is perhaps the only constant in the realm of human experience. In it, what is begun must be begun again and again, if a beginning
is to stand the test of time.

The stop neutralizes a tendency of percipient energy to animate
intellectual categories through which events are viewed. Assumptions
about a world external to the perceiver are neutralized. Containment of
energy within the organism activates channels ("nerve nodes") through
which moves an awareness of the other aspect of twofoldness. Resensi-
tized, the body's percipient membrane registers its own state—it grows
proprioceptive—but not only its own state. Organic awareness records
an inner state of the body with respect to a specific factor: presence or
absence of an energy life that in itself is not organic. The organism's
own awareness of itself is as a tracing of the other—a nonorganic other.

Once percipient energy does not go *out*, it is more available to
events within the organism. Even this statement is misleading. Surface
is perceived quite differently from the two standpoints, the intellectual
and the organic. In mental apperception of a surface, surface discon-
nects. It is a boundary, dividing line, and limit. It is what encloses the
interior, thereby separating it from exterior. Though contiguous with
both outer and inner, the surface, by this very contiguity, ensures that
the one does not mix with the other. Surface is impermeable and

impenetrable, a wall, an armor, a casing, a gulf. From the organic point of view, surface connects. It rejoins inside with outside with a gesture of embrace—rejoins, I say, since they are already joined. Surface is a joining—in the image of a Möbius strip, a surface that gathers outside and inside with the memory of a different sort of connectivity. Sur-face is inter-face. Surface is a reminder of relation, a tangible sign of the fact that inner and outer mutually penetrate each other and that the distinction is a functional convenience. Surface is a concentrated meeting ground, a place where centrifugal and centripetal tendencies are momentarily held in balance. Surface is where the organism perceives.

It is more accurate to say that through the action of the stop, the surface of perception comes alive. Experientially, the surface is a region of freshness. What comes to the surface is new in being newly exposed or unearthed material. Surface is a sensitive membrane, the only place at which growth is possible. That its existence is at risk of rigidification or deadening means that surface is forever threatened with death. When it lacks flexibility to respond to the present time, surface has already become encrusted with thickening layers of concept, idea, and assumption—with the known. Encrusted, it grows deadened. It insulates and protects against the changing time, that is, against perception. Surface ceases to connect elements and becomes a shield against connections.

It is different when the stop arrests the attention. Fresh surface (a pleonasm) gets exposed in the same way that surface is geologically exposed: by shock. Arrest is abrupt, sharp, and brute. Eruption, sudden cleavage, collapse, violent breaking, or unexpected collision compels the attention to awareness. There is a shift from passivity to activity to face the unknown. There are gentler shocks too, in paradox (for the mind) or conflict (for the feelings.) In all cases, shock exposes. This makes it, as Peirce remarks, a volitional idea. The stop is volitional in the double sense that it exposes both the willfulness of projective habits and the willingness of a twofoldness of perception. As a result of shock, both self-will and a preparedness to follow a higher authority surface.

Peirce also notices that shock implies a resistance. There must exist a force counter to the shock. Shock is a direct confrontation with another force that, through that confrontation, draws the line of battle. Until shock, a resisting force operates submerged in the field of perception, not felt or seen. Shock brings resistance to the surface. It makes it apparent that resistance is and has been at work. Thus, shock is the context for revealing what lies hidden in the depths. Shock is the discoverer of resistance, its treasure. Shock instantly recognizes the meaning of resistance and seeks effortfully to delineate the other current, reentering the organic habitat. The delineation marks the surface of which I speak.

Surface appears behind the face of habit that projects the world *out-there* and keeps it out-there, held disengaged by the category of permanence from the perceiver. Surface, the face behind the face, meets habit as a resistance. Surface in itself is effort, that which encounters resistance in its very being. Or what amounts to the same thing, the point of effort is to bring to the surface what lurks in the shadows. When surface is not confused with the outer skin, it stretches to varying depths, depending (as we might expect) on the intensity, duration, and precision of the effort. Sometimes surface is located just at or under the skin. Other times it seems to encompass a volume of a part of, or the whole of, the organism. Other times, it has a concentration or is more or less diffuse. The fact that surface varies in depth differentiates it from "surface" as a mental category.

The stop brings awareness back to the surface, out of hiding. Surface is where perception takes place. Surface is the membrane that places the organism in contact with reality. Contact remains a potential until the attention is contained within the organism. It is in response to the attention on the body that surface reappears.

The advent of surface marks an important transition. Sur-face (literally "on the face") reintroduces a missing uniqueness in perception. Surface alerts us to the fact that organic experience wears a face, and "face" belongs primarily to a person, and not just any person. The structure of the organism endows perception with a sense of belonging—belonging to myself. For the face of perception that appears is no nameless face but my own. Sur-face makes perception *mine* in the sense that it is essentially a perception of *myself*.

My face is reflected on the face of things. The moon has a face, or an animal, a cloud, a rock, a tree stump, or a wisp of smoke, only because my perception is through and of a face. The face is the frame. The face is related to the person as sign is to hidden meaning. Reading a face, I come up with a person's integrity, virtue, despair, or deceit. I experience how surface opens organically to depth, how the two, in being related, share what is similar. The similar is the unique element. It is the *who* of a situation that faces both ways, toward what is expressed explicitly and what is only hinted at implicitly. It is, in Paracelsus's phrase, the treasure marked by the features of a face.

A face-to-face meeting can bring me back to a forgotten potentiality. A background element in my perception comes forth—myself. Who the perceiver is enters the sur-face of perception by way of enrichment, and sur-face in turn adds form to the undifferentiated source energy from which it arises. When I am met by the other person, the sur-face might, at varying depths, intermingle. I and the other might be interpenetrated by one and the same set of influences. Our separate uniquenesses, through contiguity of time and space, share an understanding. Part of understanding concerns the face that sur-face does not exclude but joins.

Sur-face is not a threshold I enter to get to the heart of the place. Sur-face is the accomplishment of making entrance. The one who greets me is the one whom I have been, without knowing it, looking for. Sur-face is the enactment of my meeting myself.

Organism and Divination

In the stop, the body surfaces. In the arrest of energy that follows the pathway of habituation, intellectual construction of the world comes to a stop. A second pathway appears and, in order to be sustained, invites a conscious repetition of the stop. It passes in a direction opposite to the first and brings forth the organism from hidden folds. As channels open, a sensitive network starts to resonate to influences distant and near, local and global, subtle and audacious. Perception lies wholly with maintaining the resonant circuit, not in any outward-seeking regard. For when the circuitry is correctly attuned, the organic sensitivity picks up a vibratory energy from the presence of the world—and, more than the world, the cosmos. It is this capacity that Descartes ascribes to the blind man, who is able to "distinguish the presence of trees, stones, sand, water, grass, mud, etc."

Yet even this way of putting it compounds a misperception. To use the metaphor of transmission—a signal being broadcast and received—is already to regard "surface" as barrier and limit, that is, as an intellectual construct. For the selfsame reason, Marcel's argument against what he calls the "message theory of perception" is both promise and misstep. Marcel points out that the traditional view of perception takes a signal in the image of a transmission from object to receiver, the subject. How object transmits its signal is unclear, and so is how subject is to translate it back into object language. The signal differs radically in kind from the translation. What spans the gap but the act of reading? The message theory secrets away the role of interpretation, disguising imaginative play under the mask of mechanized translation. No such mechanism exists. Perception at its heart involves a confrontation of imagination with text. From the conjunction arises the peculiar act of perceiving what is.

However persuasive Marcel's argument against the message theory may be, the very frame contradicts its conclusion. If a transmission from outer to inner is inadmissible as a conclusion, it is also inadmissible as a hypothesis. Perception, as initiated by the stop, involves reference not to a world *out there*, but to a sensitive surface marked with text. The supposed difference between signal and translation—the metaphor of transmission—reiterates the difference between text and interpretation, more a kinship than a difference. Interpretation becomes a part of a wider text that includes primary text and commentary, all as one. That perception occupies a moment in the examination of the "surface markings" before it becomes part of the surface does not claim for it any special inner status.

When perception has an organic basis, it is of indications. What is indicated, as with "surface markings"—a deeper meaning—has an important peculiarity. The surface is that of myself. The signs are of my own reality. They reveal a secret identity through revealed meanings of events befalling me. That secret identity is myself. The unfolding text of organic perception is self-disclosure. The means by which the unknown "I" becomes manifest is reading the text of perception.

Divination is nothing but self-disclosure of the text of perception.

The one who divines the meanings of signs has the position of being a witness to the process. The seer does not decipher, decode, or demystify a given text. It is text that unriddles itself. The seer is privy to the unriddling in the unique position he or she occupies. By abstaining from marking or unmarking the text, the seer watches the unfolding surface of perception and the events, present and not present, that it tells. To the extent that perceiver is aware of relations to other lives, what is read takes on a universality. Divination is less an act of perceiving and more an act of witnessing perception.

The one who divines hidden meanings expresses understanding of an archaic language. Certain natural languages once incorporated the same peculiar feature that the *arche*-language did. Grammatically, such a language parses every action into the reflexive. "I see a road" becomes by this grammar "I see myself a road." "I hear a bird" becomes "I hear myself a bird," "I touch a table" becomes "I touch myself a table," and "I taste cinnamon" becomes "I taste myself cinnamon." The syntactical insight derives from a recognition of a factor hidden in the relation the perceiver has with the perceived. Whatever I perceive assists in revealing a secret identity for which my ordinary identity is a sign. My role as witness is signified by the reflexive construction. To rephrase Berkeley, to perceive is to be myself perceived.

The stop makes perceptive surface come alive. What comes to the surface is a hidden identity that I, without knowing it, am. Since I attend to perception as a witness, it can be said that I am attendant to my own birthing. Through repetition of the act of perceiving in the organic dimension, the submerged "I" who appears reflexively is gradually brought to full existence. The process at each moment remains unperfected. There always remains a fuller perfection with which to qualify existence. The reflexive construction is never superseded.

Divination and Time

When the stop arrests the intellectualizing tendencies of the mind, the concept of time is also affected. Time is ordinarily understood through succession (one event follows another), direction (movement from past to future), insufficiency ("Never enough time"), and extraneousness (being outside of and containing events.) When time comes to a stop, one experiences, not timelessness, but time unqualified by intellect. In the new order, the a priori form of intuition (Kant) or internal time sense (Husserl) gives way to an organic apprehension of the present moment. A reversal of ordinary assumptions takes place. Events are linked by nonlinear relations rather than by succession. Time ceases to be past, present, and future, and instead either moves or is frozen. Time becomes ample enough to allow an event to occur without crimping it. Time ceases to exist apart from what takes place; instead, it becomes a quality specific to that event.

Abolition of extrinsic time recalls perception to a temporal sense that predates abstraction and substantive generality. The organism meets time as pulse, rhythm, and tempo. Time is a paramount practical concern that governs locomotion, coordination, and the manipulation of tools. For embodied intelligence, there is no concern any more important. Thus does time give way to timing.

When it is said that time is a quality intrinsic to what takes place, *timing* is meant. Timing has to do with the time a thing, process, or result moves in. Slow or retarded, swift or accelerated, impeded or free, timing determines a thing's availability to relations with itself and others. Timing is what allows gears to mesh or, failing that, allows cataclysmic accidents to happen. Though each thing moves in its own time, how different times join or disjoin is the principal province of timing. Timing is a most intimate reflection of relation since it has everything to do with harmonizing tempos, joining movements-in-progress, adjusting rhythms, and respecting the beat. As soon as we see the cosmos as an orderly arrangement of things, events, and processes of different tempos, timing becomes the great hidden meaning. Who knows the timing of things holds the key to power. Hamlet, who knows many things, knows precious little about timing. Because of a gap in his education, he meets his doom.

The matter of engagement raises questions of timing. Timing tells when to begin and when to end, when to open and when to close. It tells what is enough and what is too much. It tells what can be entered more deeply and what must be postponed. Imprecision in timing can cause an explosion where right timing would have brought an embrace. Good timing can win fame and fortune. Bad timing might lose an empire or one's life. When it comes to telling the tale, timing can make the most interesting banal or the most trivial interesting. In the field of action, timing is a factor that enters every aspect, large and small. To be aware of it is to know what to do, how, when, and in what manner.

Returning perception to an organic membrane that communes with reality, the stop discloses timing. Time in the singular is revealed as an abstraction. With a thing, process, or event, there is no single time, overarching each and every aspect, but many. There is a time *for* meeting, a time *for* falling in love, a time *for* marrying, and a time *for* begetting. As Paracelsus, who studies the dynamics of timing, says, "time does not run in one way, but to many thousand ways. For you see that thyme blooms all the year round, whereas the crocus has its time in autumn."[1] Each thing, process, or event is a nexus of tempos, a cluster of rhythms responding to different influences. The deeper knowledge of organic perception pertains to potential times or timings of an object.

Yet the hidden focus of perception remains the same. The disclosure of the one who perceives—myself—is time's forgotten concern. "What kind of time is it for me?" is a way of asking after the identity who needs to engage. Who I am is shown me largely though facts of timing. I notice a revolving door in front of me. When I mistime it, the shock reveals my preoccupations, hesitancy, or fear. A kind of mental activity has captivated me. My lack of poise is revealing. In fact, shocks themselves are the address of timing. I am caught unawares, unprepared, with feet flat, off-balance, without proper dress, and with my hair down. I am brought once again to attest to my imperception. Inattentive to timing, I have collided with the door.

A shock is an unplanned for, fortuitous occurrence. That it is unpredictable is to say that it does not fit into the intellectual frame in which perception is habitually kept. Accidents (scalding myself with coffee), chance events (overhearing a crime being plotted or finding a ten dollar bill), slips of the tongue (saying "sad" instead of "mad"), and coincidences (meeting M the morning after I dreamed of her) disclose the yet-unrevealed depths of an identity that I unknowingly am. They are volitional in the second sense of Peirce, namely, they come in response to a felt need to perceive myself. Such shocks might be unwanted by self-will, but by a will to embody myself they are welcome, even solicited. In a sense, they are attracted to my life by an unknown identity as a means of making itself (myself) perceived.

Accident, chance, and coincidence are broad avenues through which a larger will communicates with the smaller one. The text is shocking in the same way that catching myself unprepared in a mirror is. What I perceive is undeniably the one I am constantly denying that I am—myself. What accident, chance, and coincidence share in common is their timing. The chance words in Descartes's dream ("Est et non"), Curie's fortuitous discovery of radioactivity, or the coincidental meeting of Einstein and Schweitzer are similar in text. They forcibly bring to an end an old chain of events and ring in the new. They form an interface of one time with another in which an uneasy transition must nonetheless be undergone. Accident, chance, and coincidence represent changes in time when a new influence throws off all established timing.

Timing is the great vehicle through which self-disclosing perception operates. Great knowledge attends to timing. Able to perceive how the season changes, a farmer reads the signs and knows what seed to plant. Able to perceive how the market moves, an entrepreneur reads the signs and knows what commodity to sell. Able to perceive how the heart feels, a person reads the signs and knows where well-being lies. To know the time is to know what obstacles impede movement of all kinds and to be able to take steps accordingly. Knowing the time of rain, one carries an umbrella. Not knowing the time of flood, one falls into a ditch, full of flood waters.

On the Use of Method in Divination

The extraordinary demand of divinatory perception on the attention has led to a search for a more methodical approach. We have seen the role the stop plays. A disciplined awareness combined under favorable conditions can read the text of the world. Because of the inadequacy of any sufficient condition, a quest for divinatory perception must be as a by-product of a larger aim. Reading signs is secondary to the primary pursuit of Self. The effort at attention that can uncover a sign serves a purpose of its own. The end is self-knowledge.

Whether effort yields a perceptive surface to register a meaningful event is beyond a perceiver's control. To vouchsafe a reading, different cultures in almost every historical period have devised an orderly framework in which the chance element can enter and operate for divinatory purposes. A book of oracles is created. The forms may be pictorial, numerical, symbolic, or themselves objects. Combinations of elements are generated by indeterminacy. With each combination is associated a piece of divinatory text ("the oracle"). It is up to a reader to interpret the combination, the passage in text, or both with respect to a specific situation. The acuity of a reader's commentary is the methodological replacement for a percipient awareness of the world, as already discussed.

An example that employs a method of divination is the *I Ching*, a title usually translated as *The Book of Changes*, but more nearly meaning *The Book of Transformations*. Dating from the archaic period, the *I Ching* incorporates a binary system that uses lines, unbroken and broken, to represent light and dark, strong and weak, masculine and feminine. Lines are grouped into trigrams, and each of the eight possible combinations is said to represent a sign and is assigned a meaning. To achieve greater multiplicity, the trigrams are doubled, yielding sixty-four possible hexagrams. Each of the six lines of a hexagram is generated by chance occurrences. A reading is associated with the character of each hexagram.

Typically, one comes to the *I Ching* with a question concerning a given situation. The hexagram (or hexagrams) generated then represents a sign of the meaning hidden in a situation. The reading invites interpretation on the part of a person consulting the *I Ching*. The act of reading—of seeing connections on the percipient surface of the organism—is divinatory perception. One sees that a sign is meant for oneself in the sense of offering specific information on the engagement and the timing of an undertaking. One is given to divine a course of action.

I decided to consult the *I Ching's* system of divination about a particular question. The question asked about the validity of method in the exercise of divinatory perception. Was there a fixed frame whose elements permitted a free play of such perception?

Using traditional yarrow sticks, I generated the hexagrams *Kou* (Coming to Meet) and *Ku* (Work on What Has Been Spoiled [Decay].) *Kou* especially interested me because it describes a situation in which the light triumphs only to find that the dark has unexpectedly and furtively reentered from below and within. Though the dark is weak, it is a time when the light is magnetized by and attracted to it, lending it power. The situation is described as "unfavorable and dangerous." The judgment associated with *Kou* states: "The maiden is powerful/One should not marry such a maiden."[2]

Analysis of the meaning of this cryptic statement yielded little of substance. The key to its meaning seemed lacking, yet just around the corner. The contradictory situation gave me pause, so that in one moment a relation to a deeper signification became apparent. The hexagram provided a response to my question. It told me that method (like a maiden) in divinatory perception is a powerful attraction that must be watched with great care. The impulse to rely on method (to "marry" it) is strong. The attraction of method is its easy availability. It gives itself over to whomever calls upon it. In the hexagram, the single dark line surrenders itself to the other five light lines. Method thus appears to be a replacement of the unpredictable event that is its perceived sign itself. The hexagram cautions strongly against accepting such a methodological replacement.

The danger of method is that it easily gives over to mechanical replacement. This is the marriage in which the power of divinatory perception is seized by the wily ways of the rational mind. Words themselves provide a gloss of meaning. Method thus nips perception of correspondence in the bud. In fact, method in itself never provides more than a frame in which the text of divination may appear. The frame may remain empty in the way that an easy marriage remains barren. The work of divination lies in preparation: the effort to stop the linear, discursive, explanatory mode and return to an organic awareness of things. The danger of method lies in an abandonment of that preparation.

The Presence of the World

The form that the stop lends to perception is of the organism. Percipient energy animates a sensitive kinesthetic surface rather than an intellectual frame. Two sides of the surface appear, the body's cavity and the world, but, like on a Möbius strip, there is really only one. When surface is activated, events it registers have apparent locations on one or the other side. But the difference is only in the connections events enjoy on one and the same surface, whether they are nearer to or farther from a focal point. Written on the surface is a text in which the "markings" of sensation can be read as indications of the presence of the world. This is one way to understand the doctrine of correspondence, similarity, or harmony that was so prevalent in traditional circles of Descartes's era.

For purposes of divination, the correspondence sooner goes the other way. Perceived events take on a divined meaning intended solely for whoever perceives the secret similarity. "It is a message meant only for me." This is part of their secretness. Their meaning belongs to the perceiver, and to the perceiver alone, not simply for being at the right place at the right time. What can be communicated to another lacks the incommunicable, third aspect that makes a sign's meaning triadic. Our communication tries to replace the third with a second or binary sign. Because secretness consists in being addressed by the world, it is strictly irreplaceable. For this reason, divination in its primary and principal occurrence has a first-person referent. Only in derivative usages does it take on forms of interpersonal communication, in which someone plays the role of the diviner. More precisely, no one can play that role who is not involved in the meaning itself—though others can catalyze divination, as did the pythoness of the Delphic oracle.

What is the secret content of the sign? It has to do with the specificity of timing. This involves two kinds of specifics. First, timing tells what to do when, in what way, and with what approach. It concerns the specifics of engagement. Second, the meaning tells of the one whose time it is. It deals with the specifics of identity. Divinatory perception brings a momentary contact with a forgotten memory. Such memory is not of the past but of the present. The meaning of a divination is secret because a lost aspect of a perceiver is rediscovered. Having been buried, it is protected from kinds of distortion to which conceptual memory is susceptible. This is reason for secrecy. Divinatory perception takes place only when perception's susceptibility to lying has been eliminated. In time, perception remembers a relation between what presently occurs and what is to come.

The fact that secret meaning can be distorted by "subjective untruths" raises an important question of verification. It would, however, be too hasty to conclude that verification consists, as it does in binary signs, of repeatability. An outstanding virtue of binary signs is their publicity or intersubjectivity. *Red* means a patch of redness to all who perceive it. When there is a challenge to a perception of redness, the means of adjudication lie in a second look, preferably someone else's. Reidentification of the red patch settles the matter once and for all. It is otherwise with triadic meaning. The third aspect of meaning— the relation that holds between the sign and the signified—appears only when the two surfaces of perception correspond harmonically to become one. Just as with a Möbius strip, there is a "twist" in the direction of things that eliminates dualities. Meaning returns to an archaic form in which difference-making events take place in the world and the subject at once, without being in two different locations.

The correspondence that remains confined to what I have called the "percipient surface" tangibly relates the *who* to the *what* of perception. It blends subjective with objective to create a new aspect different from but inclusive of both. Since the surface depends on the rigorous condition of organic attentiveness, its life is confined to the moment. So too with triadic meaning and its secret revelation. Thus, its verification differs from that of repeatability.

The delicate matter of verifying divinatory perception, combined with its fallibility, has led thinkers to dismiss it as unverifiable altogether. It wears aspects of a private language, one only the perceiver can decipher. The collapse of triadic into binary meaning, moreover, is an outcome of Descartes's treachery. Although it might have served his project well, triadic meaning was effectively eliminated when he turned—in the name of a new democratic spirit—to an object language. Truth thereby shifted from the correspondence of the one reading the text to the veracity of the text itself in which one sign mirrors another in ceaseless representation of text to itself. It shifted from how deeply a reader resonated to the play of the world to how accurately copied one sign was for another. It shifted from correspondence to coherence.

Verification of divinatory perception has to do with the activation of a special kind of memory. To the extent to which what one divines by a specific perception is verifiable, to that extent one remembers an identity hidden behind all perception. The import and intent of divination is to bring to light what remains obscure in the subject of divination, the *who*. When I divinatorily perceive what is occurring, I see what is happening in light of what is to come *and* I see myself. The dimension of verifiability derives from the peculiar conjunction of events, not the one or the other. That I remember myself renders divinatory perception immune to claims of arbitrariness or false imagination.

The ultimate ground of perception lies in this special memory. When active, the memory, felt as an organic presence, remembers the person from which acts issue yet who does not engage in action. When active, memory assures that a perceiver is *in* the time that corresponds to the present. Thus, this memory most assuredly is not a memory of the past, of events that once took place and now may be represented to thought. Memory that makes assumptions about oneself must be gone beyond if the special memory is to found. The memory in question, moreover, is not of what is happening or about to happen, as though these two modes were species of remembered events. Instead, it is not of any time in particular or in general, but of the matter of timing. It is memory of poise and the stop.

What is remembered by memory of timing? It is not the content of this time or that, be it past, present, or future. Such content tells what has happened, is happening, or will happen. It relates to tense. Timing relates otherwise. It relates to engagement. When timing is remembered, one remembers laws of engaging. One remembers how to join in. Participation, availability, and initiation are aspects of this memory. Divinatory perception is a by-product of the cultivation of a memory of timing.

A memory of timing is different from a memory of time. Timing is about time relations, not about specific times. Remembering timing, one might know nothing about *what* is to happen. Knowing how *this* moment relates to *that*, one knows when, how, and in what manner to engage the act. Plausibly, one can do this while ignorant of specific outcomes. A dancer or gymnast, embodying an awareness of time relations, is able to perform in a way that expresses an inner geometry of nearness and power. When one does not have a sense of time relations, one's particular acts remain disjointed, ineffectual, without a point, without an author. Time relations, in turn, are the actual relations of the surface of perception, the connections between one event and another. Proficiency in an organic awareness that yields perceptual moments also develops a sense of timing. Practice in the stop leads to a memory of timing, which in turn leads back to the stop.

Finally, a memory of the perceiver—myself—leads to and joins with a memory of timing. Remembering myself is less like recalling an object, with its string of properties somehow inhering in its substance, to mind, and more like striking up a melodic rhythm again. The two differ principally in the temporal dimension. The essence of an object is timelessness, that of myself, timeliness. The object's appearance depends on an atemporal conceptual frame, whereas I make my appearance only in accordance with the strictly enforced conditions of timing that allow it. The way to remembering myself proceeds through pulse, heartbeat, and synaptic nerve firings, all being timed phenomena. The fullness of memory amplifies these preliminary indications of timing and adjusts them like a conductor to a harmonious symphony of effects, to a single melodic rhythm carried by a multitude of sources. Recognition of such time relations—stops, starts, repetitions, echoes, overtones, undercurrents—permits an appreciation of the complexity of matters of timing.

6

Sight and Movement

The Cane of the Blind

Some while ago, we abandoned Gloucester, recently blinded by Regan, on the way to Dover. Him we left with a pressing question. The question had a tone quite different from those of philosophers beset by various puzzles about the blind's perception. Those questions are self-serving. They reinforce the already reinforced frame of concepts defining the world of the sighted. Our question concerns the oppressed and outcast. It is important for us all to understand the means by which the blind can find their way.

The figure of Descartes lends his authority to the modern view. The figure, as I have pointed out, is an ambiguous one. Descartes's is an intricate project, an exercise in subterfuge and disguise, a bold and daring attempt to establish a new intellectual order. Moreover, it appears to be what it is not, and it is not at all as it appears. Descartes's apparent paean to sight, his geometrization of vision, camouflages his real intent. He puts on the categories of sightedness to wear the cloak of knowledge, but his aim is more radical. He wants to overthrow the authority of sight, the old masters of philosophy, and to install a new thralldom—of the blind. While I have not examined in depth Descartes's motives, the reasons for his rebelliousness, I have stressed the importance of revenge. Feeling himself emotionally and intellectually blinded by traditional ways of thinking—which he deems to be ways of the spiritually elite—he is driven by vengeance to remake the edifice of knowledge. Thus, he steps into the role of a Hamlet, a Saturnian earth-shaker who will murder his forebears in order to bring insurrection to a successful climax.

To step into a Hamlet role is audacious. It is also fraught with risk. It suits Descartes as Hamlet not to act transparently. This fact should warn us that his strategies require careful deciphering. But there is a dual risk attending an archetypal role. Descartes is first at risk in that the role will play him rather than the reverse. We need look only to Hamlet to see this happen. Hamlet, himself brilliant, falls prey to the dilatory habits of the fool he plays. Descartes also succumbs to this risk. Consumed by the Hamlet role, he loses track of what he wants to accomplish and fails in his purpose of establishing the hegemony of the blind. Inattentive to the stop, he is derailed by it and botches his job.

The second risk is infatuation. Hamlet's fatal attraction to his disguise makes it impossible for him to discard it at the proper time. Too many mannerisms, postures, intonations, and props have become attached to him. Freedom to act on behalf of himself has been impaired. Descartes likewise compromises his project by attachment to the blind man's role. Lack of clarity emerges in one important specific. This detail is present from the very first introduction of the blind-man character. It is the cane. The blind man's cane trips up Descartes's project.

The cane is for Descartes a symbol of blindness. Lacking an outward-seeking sense of sight and its effortless leap across space, the blind find consolation in a little stick and use it for guidance. The stick is humble and commonplace. Reach down anywhere along the way and there is something to serve as a cane. A found object, it has no special composition or structure, no intrinsic value. It is a natural object, whereas blindness (in the paradigmatic case I consider) is inflicted by humans. Nature graciously provides the blind with the stick as meager compensation for their loss. It by no means equals the face value of impairment, since sight is irreplaceable, an infinite sum that cannot be balanced. The stick improves the lot of the blind, but at the same time it expresses impoverishment rather than dignity, hopelessness rather than worth, ignorance rather than knowledge. It announces itself as a partial solution to an insoluble problem, a tokenism forced upon its user. The blind use a cane because poverty in their situation compels it, not because they choose to.

As a symbol, the cane stands for oppression and servility, ineptitude and dehumanization. It oppresses in that the blind are under its power. Take away their canes, and they are powerless to move. The cane brings out the servile nature of the blind inasmuch as they rely on it for the simplest acts of location or retrieval. It demonstrates how incapable they are of accomplishment and contention in the world. With cane in hand, the blind can be read as less than human. The cane is the scourge of blindness made visible, a visible reminder that to blind is to punish. How are the blind ultimately punished? Most mortally. If the seeing eye is gateway to the soul, does not the blind eye clinch the proof of a soulless being?

The cane is patently antagonistic to Descartes's hidden purpose of empowering the blind's peculiar mode of perception. Even though the cane connotes irreplaceability—since it represents the sight that can never be made up for—still Descartes does not neglect the cane at every appearance. Even the famous scene in Discourse VI (which Descartes graces with a woodcut illustration) portrays a blind man with cane. Why does he place himself in contradiction?

Natural limits to a sympathetic exploration of sightlessness prevent Descartes from an unfettered pursuit of his goal. Upon discovery of the stop, Descartes does not capitalize on his newfound poise. He remains a person who sees as the sighted and looks upon the blind as the other, the outcast, the pariah. He is enthusiastic about the stop yet values an external symbol over the blind's ownmost way of perception. His vision is limited by his brief exposure to novelty.

This interpretation is too ingenuous. A cane can be an instrument by which to probe the world, or it can be a crutch. A crutch is used to gain support in lieu of standing on one's own two feet. Descartes uses the cane as a crutch to support his notion of how the eye sees.

More than the infancy of discovery, however, inhibits Descartes. Descartes wants to advertise how light moves in order to propound a favorite theory of visual perception. Once again in the Hamlet role, he must rebel against received ideas. Thus he rejects both the extramission theory (that visual force originates in the visual object) and the intromission theory (that this force originates in the eye) and also a hybrid of the two. All presuppose a passage of vibratory energy across empty space, which is objectionable to him. If a vibration is to move, it must move *through* some body: the cane is a model for this. Thus he avers that light from an object is transmitted to the retina in a manner similar to how felt resistance to an object is transmitted along the blind man's cane to the hand.

Descartes, however, fails to see the complicated triadic arrangement in which the cane plays a crucial role.

illuminated object	resisting object
x	cane
eye	hand that feels

Just as the cane is available to relate object and hand, so too does the unknown x relate visual object and eye. How does the relation go? Descartes conceives it in literal or binary terms. The cane is a channel for the "fluid" of vibratory energy. The vibration created by a collision of cane and object passes through the funnel and into the hand, where it is felt, i.e., "the movement or resistance of the bodies a blind man encounters is transmitted to his hand through his stick." Though an artificial extension of a body, the cane serves perception by conducting vibratory energy from outer world back to sensitive nerves of the palm and fingers.

When it comes to identifying x, Descartes describes it as a "luminous body." We could call it ethereal substance or simply the ether. Similar to the cane, it is a conductor of light—"a certain very rapid and lively movement or activity"—from visual object to eye. It conducts light, as does the cane a coarser vibration, by passing it segment by segment, molecule by molecule, in a direct, continuous, and linear fashion. Physical proximity and contiguity in time and space allow two segments to fall under a similar influence and ultimately to give passage to the vibration. As one domino's fall influences movement of the next, so too light falling on the eye from the sun moves under similar laws.

But it is not the influence of similars that interests Descartes's thinking. The linearity of old tradition—the linear of Euclid's *Optics*— still dominates thought. Gnarled, crooked, or gently bowed, the cane is seen as linear in function. The vibratory impact initiated by collision simply repeats a straight line. A rock-to-hand trajectory is always straight because the cane can instigate no new pathway. Linearity, more than any other element dictates thought, overworks it, and eventually overthrows it. Descartes avoids asking the ways in which cane, hand, and object are similar, as similar they must be.

The cane, understood triadically, is a sign for a deeper meaning of the hand's percipience, really, the body's. Watch how a blind person wields a cane. The cane moves with a shifting intent, not in a straight line. It reaches out probingly, bumps into an object, and withdraws to one side. It then takes a new direction, swings back, bumps into the same object, and moves aside. Cane travels searchingly, with stops and starts, in jerks, pausing over questions, resolving them, needing confirmation, retiring to an aside, beginning again. The blind person's body atttentively obeys the cane's indications and walks accordingly. A correspondence exists between cane and motility to the extent that the body is the condensed intention of the cane. The cane wants to perceive what is in the way of travel. The body concentrates the selfsame impulse and muscularly actualizes it. Body and cane share a perception, but as center and perimeter. I have spoken of this form of organic perception. Swinging back and forth, to and fro, the cane seeks out obstacles before it in the road. Its way of perceiving is through resistance. Without impediments, its perception would be without content. Similarly, an organic form of perception develops only through resistance. Awareness is returned to the body: this is the stop. In the brief opening, awareness meets tension, strain, and muscular rigidity within the confines of the body. It also meets a host of attitudes toward the organic resistance. These are resistances on another level: refusal to abide in the condition of awareness, a desire to be distracted, a dislike of what is met, a liking for change. Thus, to strike a pose and take up the stop is to call forth an impulse to be unstopped. Within a space of the stop, affirmation of arrest meets its denial. Where that is all, a moment of poise is promised but not attained. If, however, awareness is able to contain both affirmation and denial, a way to perception is opened. Then the blind man can travel from here to Dover and back in a single day.

Let me return briefly to Descartes's other triad of object, luminous body, and eye. If we apply our conclusions, the luminous body no longer serves to conduct illumination from object to eye. The cane, we saw, is a sensitive extension or rarefaction of a more central organic impulse to perceive the world. Its movement along the road's surface expresses the impulse perfectly. Rock or root, by the same token, present themselves to the tip of the cane already willing to be perceived. Similarly, luminous bodies are understood as sensitive extensions of the eye's urge to see the world. The eye itself is a concentrated intention of luminous bodies to allow sight to take place. Just as organic perception arises in response to solicitations of the cane and the world, so too does perception arise from the organ of sight. One could even say, as does Goethe, that the eye as an organ evolves in response to the address of a light-filled universe.

Maine de Biran

Perception equals effort plus resistance. Subtracting effort from both sides of the equation leaves a perception that cannot reckon resistance as a factor, bodiless perception. Its degenerate Platonism views the organism as vulgar, bedeviled, and profane. Perception of the higher cannot involve the body that is barked, bruised, strained, sprained, and overexerted. Like seeing light, such perception costs nothing and travels in straight lines. The thought associated with it follows a similar route and places itself at the center of things. Its chief project is the thought construction of reality. Its lineages are nominalism and phenomenalism. It is the long tradition whose roots find fertile soil in the pre-Socratic thought that Descartes struggles against and, caught in the mill of Hamlet's overintellectualization, ultimately succumbs to. With Descartes's self-entrapment, much of modernity likewise falls victim to an illusion of effortless perception.

The stop is acknowledgment of resistance. Made conscious, the stop effortfully fills perception with body. To school thought in this direction would be to fulfill Descartes's intended project. Writing two centuries after Descartes, Maine de Biran, in his *Mémoire sur la décomposition de la pensée* (1805), recognizes the importance of a conscious encounter with resistance. He also looks to the blind man's cane. The cane exemplifies arrested movement. An acknowledgment of resistance, he shows, is effortful because

> effort carries with it the perception of a relation between the being that moves and wants to move and a certain obstacle that opposes its movement; without a subject or will that determines movement, without resistance, there is no effort, and without effort, no knowledge, and without perception, neither.[1]

The form of particular perceptions of intention and obstacle is what Maine de Biran calls "coenesthetic," namely, "the feeling of a whole composed of all vital impressions inherent in each part of the organism."[2] Coenesthesis is the fundamental or *ur*-sensation to which particular kinds of sensations (smell, sight, taste, touch, hearing) are related as part to whole. Its primordiality derives from the fact that

> it suffices to give the soul the idea of the presence of its own body and of the different parts of the body to which sensitive feelings are related in so much as they are perceived by myself (*le moi*).[3]

The stop awakens a sensitivity associated with the unique percipience that is coenesthesis. A conjunction of effort and resistance supplies the condition appropriate to discovery. Awareness is called to two
facts. Maine de Biran writes of the first:

> that it is in acting on the body itself (*le corps propre*), in as
> much as it is inert and mobile under the soul's effort, that
> the soul begins to be aware of it itself in its union with the
> body, and next, to have a feeling more or less obscure of the
> presence or the coexistence of this body.[4]

The first fact points to the second: that when unrestrained bodily movement is checked, there is an enhanced possibility to recognize that
unrestrained awareness of the blockage also is checked. Awareness of
the first fact leads to appreciation of the special relation between awareness and the organism that houses it. Awareness of the second fact
moves toward the yet-more-special appreciation that the body-soul has
a relation to an Other that relates all similars. Awareness grows cogni-
zant of relation itself.

Maine de Biran's blind man possesses the cane and, with it, coenesthetic perception, "the immediate feeling of the presence of the
body."[5] These two are really one. The cane pokes and prods along,
meeting the surface of the highway. Rocks, roots, an occasional found
article, protrude. Or perhaps the highway presents a perfectly flat and
level surface, an angelic straightaway. Each encounter of cane and pave-
ment or obstacle creates a particular dislocation in, or distortion of, the
presence of the body. To the extent that our blind man remains coenes-
thetically alert, to that extent he relies on his body's ownmost form of
perception to guide his locomotion.

Effort marks coenesthesis. On one surface of effort's percipience
appears the world—in this case, the road that stretches to the white
cliffs of Dover. On the other surface, myself, "the individual subject
('*moi*') of an effort, under the fundamental relation and necessary to the
term of organic resistance."[6] But the two surfaces are really one, though
they, like the Möbius strip, appear as two until further scrutiny. The
depth of this study, as Maine de Biran insists, is that of effort. Through
movement in the teeth of resistance alone does the membrane of
organic perception, coenesthesis, become active.

How does a blind person walk? Must one, as Regan recommends savagely to Gloucester, smell his or her way? A certain possibility—of a poised, though blind, movement—presented itself early in my demasking of Descartes. It depended on a new and acutely demanding use of the attention, a reinhabitation of the body itself. But does the possibility, while logical and cogent, belong to the sighted and not the blind when they themselves attest to their experience?

Lusseyran recently offered compelling descriptions of a way of sightlessly navigating the world. Born sighted, he became blind due to an accident while young. Unlike the Samson icon and its bitter resentment, however, he is not condemned to a life that seeks surreptitiously to avenge the blinding. "Every day since [the accident]," he writes, "I have thanked heaven for making me blind while I was still a child not quite eight years old."[7] Blinding is not punishment, deprivation, or excommunication from the fellowship of humans and God. Neither is it an event that solicits a compensatory gift, as in the case of Tieresias, a gift that accords privilege of extraordinary perception. Lusseyran is not granted powers of prophecy or divination to counterbalance what was taken from him. Instead, blinding allows Lusseyran to conduct himself in a thoroughly human way—to move freely about the world of things. Blinding is a gift in itself.

The nature of unexpected gifts is that they reveal their hidden nature unexpectedly. Lusseyran describes walking along a familiar path in a park, one day not long after his accident, longing for eyes to see. "At this point," he writes,

> some instinct—I was almost about to say a hand laid on me—made me change course. I began to look more closely, not at things but at a world closer to myself, looking from an inner place to one further within, instead of clinging to the movement of sight toward the world outside.[8]

The gift is of an awareness open to the light. Its novelty involves a shift in the angle of regard, a turn away from attending to the distant and indifferent. The new direction is that in which things of the world thenceforward show themselves as radiant rather than dark. Such attentiveness aligns itself with a source of radiance that "might as well have been outside me as within," and either way allows the world to be perceived. Its discovery, Lusseyran contends, is proof that the sighteds' picture of the blind—as stooped and stupid, groping and groveling, benighted and bestial—is itself oppressive and expressive of a campaign of oppression. The blind know themselves otherwise. He writes, "Sighted people always talk about the night of blindness. . . . But there is no such night, for at every waking hour and even in my dreams I lived in a stream of light."[9]

Lusseyran argues that, whatever effects it produces in him, the origin of nonsighted illumination is independent of his state. It is no by-product of the attempt to perceive. A properly disposed attention must be available to percipient energy. The attention either organizes the soma or allows an inherent order to manifest itself. If a functional organ is a means of organizing the data of impressions, then the shift allows the recovery of a forgotten organ of perception. Lusseryan reports in a literal way that "the seeing eye was in me." However when attention is not wholly given to the new direction, disturbances in perception take place. Negative emotional states, fear, anger, and impatience, have strongly distracting, centrifugal energies that profoundly disturb the organic tissue. Other agitation reactivates latent habits of perception and disturbs a delicately balanced attention that demarks novelty. Perception for Lusseyran depends on the force and vitality of a refocused awareness that, while in constant threat of loss, constantly returns to a promised luminousness.

A registry of sightless perception, moreover, is as rich as that of the sighted. Color, contour, texture, shading, and spatial relations belong to both the sighted and the sightless, though in different ways. Color, a case in point, illustrates this fact. Upon blinding, Lusseryan reports, "colors, all the colors of the rainbow, also survived."[10] They, as well as other "visual" qualities, appear as nuances of a basic percipience that he describes as pressure.[11]

> What the blind person experiences in the presence of an object is pressure. When he stands a before a wall he has never touched and does not now touch, he feels a physical presence. The wall bears down on him. . . . Perception then would mean entering into an equilibrium of pressure.

The testimony helps confirm Descartes's intuition of the congruence of sight and touch—though with a twist. For Descartes, pressure is transmitted linearly from the world through the blind man's cane to his nerves and brain. It passes through a surface whose two sides separate inner from outer. For Lusseyran, pressure is spontaneity that manifests in the presence of an object. Transmission implies a separation, though "surface" does not. The perceptual surface is so designed as to render inner and outer functionally, but not spatially, distinct.

Part
Three

WHAT SEEING
SEES

*And so that Good which is above all light is
called a Spiritual Light because it is an
Originating Beam and an Overflowing
Radiance, illuminating with its fullness every
Mind above the world, around it, or within it,
and renewing all their spiritual powers,
embracing them all by Its transcendent
compass and exceeding them all by Its
transcendent elevation.*
— Pseudo-Dionysius, *On the Divine Names*

7

The Light of the Stop

The Lumen Naturale

An intriguing question emerges from a study of the motives behind the *Dioptrics*. What if Descartes had not been vengefully opposed to the tradition of the sighted? Would he and all that followed from him have seen as the blind see, by the light of the stop? Would we, the human species, have been restored to the artful poise of seeing that was lost in the downfall of Oedipus?

When Descartes puts on the cloak of blindness, he discovers that the blind move by means of the stop. The exigence of their situation returns the attention to its bodily habitat, thereby activating a forgotten "organ" of perception. By the light of its percipience, the presence of the world grows legible. Its presence and the presences of things belong to one and the same surface just as my presence to myself does. In the course of his intrigue, Descartes becomes privy to this knowledge. Vengeance, however, renders all accomplishments irrelevant, save one: the destruction of its object, in this case, the edifice of the sighteds' sight. Blinded by a magnificent obsession, Descartes marks the stop and hurries on, letting drop the fruits of its great promise.

The fact gives me pause. What if he had stopped and remembered to ask after the experience? Among a host of unvoiced questions, the one that concerns me most is about the lighting of organic percipience. How is its light like the light that the sighted see? There is a corollary question, namely, by what light is their similitude perceived?

These two questions are obscured by a separate and distinct lighting phenomenon to which Descartes attends and on which he places inestimable value. He writes of a *lumen naturale*, a species of lighting by which objects are recognized for what they are. The *lumen naturale* shows itself in operation of diverse cognitive functions, sense perception, memory, imagination, and understanding. Its appearance lends an aura of infallibility to what is seen under its light. As Descartes writes, "whatever the light of nature shows me . . . is absolutely beyond doubt; for there can be no faculty, equally trustworthy with this light, to show me that such things are not true."[1] Whenever the light of nature bursts forth, that which is in its field is free from concealment, distortion, and obscurity. Hence, the *lumen naturale* provides an incomparable standard of truth for the cognitive sciences.

Prior to its application in reflective knowledge, the *lumen naturale* has a place in everyday experience. Descartes locates it in a flash of insight that reveals a nugget of knowledge of external reality. In its familiar guise, the light is intuition. "By intuition, I mean," he writes:

> not the wavering assurance of the senses, or the deceitful judgement of a misconstructing imagination, but a conception, formed by unclouded mental attention, so easy and distinct as to leave no room for doubt in regard to the thing we are understanding. It comes to the same thing if we say: It is an indubitable conception formed by an unclouded and attentive mind; one that originates solely from the light of reason.[2]

Intuition, moreover, is unabashedly cognitive in orientation. It is a natural philosopher's inkling of or hunch about how things are, raised to a level of infallibility. Who of us is not a natural philosopher when called on to deal with reality in our day-to-day affairs? Thus, "there are far more of such truths than most people observe because they disdain to turn their mind to such easy topics."[3]

In more precise formulations of the *lumen naturale*, Descartes carefully distinguishes the source from the field or fields of illumination. Behind the diversity of its workings lies a unity of action. "[T]he power of cognition," he writes,

> properly so called is purely spiritual and is just as distinct from the body as a whole as blood is from bone or a hand from an eye; and that it is a single power. Sometimes it receives images from the common sensibility [*sensus communis*] at the same time as the phantasy does; sometimes it applies itself to the images preserved in memory; sometimes it forms new images and these so occupy the imagination that often it is not able at the same time to receive

ideas from the common sensibility or pass them on to the locomotive power in the way that the body left to itself would.[4]

Or:

The cognitive power is always one and the same; if it applies itself, along with the imagination, to the common sensibility [sensus communis], it is said to see, feel, etc.; if it applies itself to the imagination alone, insofar as that is already provided with various images, it is said to remember; if it does this in order to form new images, it is said to imagine or conceive; if, finally, it acts by itself, it is said to understand.[5]

When its bounds—from memory to imagination and back to sense perception—are surveyed, the light of the light of nature seems as magical as its operation. It apparently arises on its own, from nowhere, neither invited nor caused to appear. At the same time, that which is absent, forgotten, or unsensed is suddenly in view. Its qualities, function, relations, history, and future become discernible. It gives occasion to marvel and also to ask where in nature to locate its source. When we acknowledge the boundaries of its operation, it is clear that the *lumen naturale* arises from the constitution of mind. Though its field of vision may be of body or mind, the awareness itself is strictly cognitive, mental, or intellectual. Cognitive awareness is not awareness without qualification. The qualification is that the awareness is at the disposal of the conceptual scheme. It is not yet free to perceive through the whole of the human form.

Although we are not yet close to an understanding of the light of organic percipience, it is instructive to reconsider reasons why Descartes calls a cognitive awareness *lumen*. They reveal a hidden shortcoming in his attempt to overthrow the tradition of the sighted, an inner conflict that defeats his grandiose plan for revenge. For Descartes remains unconsciously swayed by an example of analogical thinking based on the light the sighted see.

The analogy is part of the tradition of the sighted and the elitism of knowledge. It perhaps begins with Plato and travels through Plotinus and Augustine to the Neoplatonists of thirteenth-century England. The argument goes like this. Physical light, the light of the sighted, falls on objects and is reflected from their surfaces. If it is sufficiently pure and intense, when it travels to the eye and the brain, it makes objects visible. By the same token, the mind's light makes objects "visible" when it is sufficiently pure (free from the preconceptions of habit) and intense (undistractedly attentive.) Objects then appear as they are and can be understood as such. One is in a position, as Descartes stresses in the famous wax example of the *Meditations*, to read their properties off by direct inspection; for

> it must be observed that perception of the wax is not sight, not touch, not imagination; nor was it ever so, though it formerly seemed to be; it is a purely mental contemplation [*inspectio*].[6]

Most importantly, such an act of mind does not analyze, evaluate, compare, or critique what is presented to it. Descartes finds the mind to be paradigmatically at rest in the *lumen naturale*. Mind is receptive, passive, and nonconstructive. Its automatism has been arrested.

The great appeal of the analogy, however, suppresses a critical gap. The light that the sighted see is an independent source of illumination affects the eye and brings about a visual image. The eye is receptively prepared, and its degree of receptivity determines the accuracy of an image. With the *lumen naturale*, the mind, cognitive awareness, or (Descartes's preference) the understanding, both emits light and receives impressions of objects disclosed. There is no independent source whose energy affects the mind's eye by way of an image. For the analogy to function properly, either the light source (e.g., the sun) would need to see what its illumination reveals or the mind's light would need to come from a source beyond mind itself. Descartes considers neither possibility. The first contradicts his assumption of the inertness of matter. The second renders mind a derivative or secondary power and saps its viability as a first principle.

Had he been able to accept either option, Descartes would have been closer to acknowledging the peculiarities of awareness, whose surface joins rather than separates. Awareness receives at the same time as it emits. But Descartes, though seeking revenge against the sighted, has still not purged himself of redemptive, light-based thoughts. Like a Samson, his is no godless vengeance but one that is to redeem his blinded self in the sight of his Maker. Augustine expresses the relation between divine vision, light, and salvation expressive of Descartes's innermost thoughts:

> But we ought . . . to believe that the intellectual mind is so formed in its nature as to see those things which by the disposition of the Creator are subjoined to things intelligible in a natural order by a sort of incorporeal light of an unique kind: as the eye of the flesh sees things adjacent to itself in this bodily light, of which light it is made to be receptive and adapted to it.[7]

But as soon as light is the text of God, oppression and exclusivity follow. What is said in the sacred language of light appears in luminous letters to be read only by the eye that sees. Those who cannot read because of disability—the blind—are outcast, excommunicated, and condemned. Humankind is divided into those graced by knowledge of the divine text and those not. As Bacon, cited earlier, writes:

> the infusion of grace in perfectly good men is analogous to light incident directly and perpendicularly, since they do not reflect grace from themselves nor refract it from the direct path that extends along the way of perfection of life.[8]

This is the tradition of the spiritually elite. In it Descartes is caught up in the very machinations he seeks to disable.

Parenthetically, there is a question concerning the origin of the analogy. By what light can it be claimed that the light of reason is *like* the light the sighted see? Where do texts of metaphor, correspondence, sympathy, resemblance, and similitude originate insofar as they apply to light? In tradition, a solution lies in the sharing of a common origin. Plato states that the idea of the good gives "birth in the visible world to light and the author of light and itself in the intelligible world being the authentic source of truth and reason."[9] The *lumen naturale* and light are rendered similar because of ancestry, family connections, or lineage. They come from one and the same.

The analogy between the *lumen naturale* and the light the sighted see works because, stemming from the same source, both are bequeathed the same energy for their different operations. In fact, analogy is the action of similitude, rectified and geometrized—that is, made to reveal proportion and harmony between apparent dissimilars. The very statement of the analogy of light furnishes proof of a common origin and energy of the two analogues. How else can they be thought similar unless each shares in a common nature whose action reveals similars as similar, and what else could the common nature be but light? The text of similarity coincides with that of light. Similarity is the expression of the enlightened origin. Therefore, analogy and its siblings give proof of the presence of light. Like knows like because each shares in the light that illuminates both.

The grip of analogy is not weakened by claims that the light of the good *causes* the light of reason and the light the sighted see. Analogy is not supplanted but supplemented by causation. Analogy is inclusive, and even though causal thought is linear and exclusive, the embrace of analogy is irresistible. Causal chains have the simple effect of multiplying likenesses, just as branches multiply the expanse of a tree. Grosseteste devises a doctrine to serve this insight, the doctrine of the multiplication of species:

> A natural agent multiplies its power from itself to the recipient, whether it acts on sense or on matter. This power is sometimes called species, sometimes a likeness, and it is the same thing whatever it may be called.[10]

Similitude spreads in the manner in which visual light diffuses. The fact is anticipated in that the latter is the visible sign of the former just as the latter is the deep meaning of the former. Sign and signified are forever bound together by the signature of light.

Furthermore, causality in general is the steward of likeness, not its master. That tradition respects a principle of similarity of cause and effect cannot be underestimated. Only like can cause like. Only like can be caused by like. For Descartes, in his blinded state, such a principle guarantees correspondences between idea and actuality. Having thrown over the cloak of blindness, his sole protection against an unreal phantasy of image and association is the rule of similars. "And though one idea," he writes,

> may originate from another, an infinite regress here is impossible: we must at last get back to some primary idea whose cause is as it were an archetype, containing actually

any reality whatever that occurs in the idea representatively.[11]

He goes on to aver that "by the light of nature the ideas in me are like pictures."[12] The *lumen naturale* is able to vouchsafe correspondence between the mental and the actual world because it itself is expressive of similitude and because similitude is its authentic expression. To say that mental ideas are *like* (rather than *are*) pictures, moreover, is to make a statement true of a logic of similars, whose speech is correspondence, rather than that of a logic of dissimilars, whose speech is existence.

The light of reason reveals for Descartes the great resemblances—principally causal ones—that have lain hidden in the bosom of darkness. Lurching forward on his blind man's cane, he passionately embraces each resemblance as a succor to his benighted state. How else can truth be ascertained from illusion? Little does he suspect, however, that revealed likenesses derive from the same philosophical elitism he desires to overthrow. How likeness follows from likeness, branching causal chains like rays of light, leading from sightless imagination to the real of the real! What seems to be a solution to a blinded subjectivism conceals the same ancient agenda of geometrizing light. Grosseteste makes this confusion explicit when he writes that "all causes of natural effects must be expressed by means of lines, angles and figures, for otherwise it is impossible to grasp their explanation." He concludes:

> Hence these rules and principles and fundamentals having been given by the power of geometry, the careful observer of natural things can give the causes of all natural effects by this method.[13]

To establish causal lines of events is to create a matrix by which the geometer is again master. Geometric optics once more provides a standard by which all similitude is judged. Descartes's great plan of liberation in the end circles back on its own tail.

The natural light of reason arrests the mind. From where does it come? Thought, having come to a stop, concerns itself with presence rather than origin. It takes in what it meets in itself. A second question arises: What is the effect of lighting on the stop itself? For the action of light is distinct from its result. That light differs in duration, intensity, breadth of focus, and warmth is not a factor in the stop but might affect one's availability to the action. The *lumen naturale* abruptly ends the intellect's automatic processing, its use of comparison, evaluation, explanation, analysis, or calculation. Arrest is the action of light. Whether an impression of the stop is allowed in, however, depends on two things: the properties of light and the aspirations of the heart. The *lumen naturale* flashes far more frequently than is noticed. Its strength, duration, brightness, or breadth might affect one's receptivity to it. But one's attitude toward the phenomenon in question dictates an interest. Descartes takes note of the second factor when he writes that, though arrest takes place often enough, people "disdain to turn their mind to such easy topics."

What arrests habitual mental operations is in the mind but not of it. A great attraction of the *lumen naturale* is that it is unthought. It energetically descends to ordinary mind from a more conscious level of intelligence. This level includes ego consciousness—which has preoccupied the Cartesian tradition—and implicit relations to reality on different levels. The light of reason, because it is awakened, awakens thought and stirs novelty. It opens the mind framed by the conceptual scheme to its origin, and from its origin, to the question of how it relates to the light itself.

The mind, when acted on by light, is no longer detained by a fixed frame of thought-constructs. It ceases to be hidden in a conceptual cloak, donned for disguise when it set off on its youthful adventure of vengeance. Under the cloak, preoccupation grows big with the future of destroying the old, established, received, accepted mode of thinking. But to act? Lacking a connection to time, thought remains supremely hesitant, dilatory, deferring, procrastinating, and ineffectual. Its hold on the reins of action is impractical and unpracticed. Under its disguise, its grip becomes rigid, taking on a permanence of its own. Thus it perpetuates the very thing it seeks to annihilate.

Light that penetrates the intellectualism immediately loosens the ossified grip. Novelty—the network of unmediated relations—is an immediate result of relaxation. Freeing mind from thought-constructs opens the greater whole of the person. A dynamic, rhythmic, and energetic experience of emerging order can be maintained only as long as it is attentively submitted to. As soon as a reflex to grasp takes over, lighting rapidly fades. A residual impression—which abandons time to timelessness—is accepted as truth. As a permanent record it is quickly incorporated into the established frame of ideas.

The Body's Light

I want to return to the question posed earlier: How is the light of the body—that which shines forth in the stop—like the light the sighted see? Since Gloucester, though blind, is able to make his way to Dover, the body's light, like the eye's for the sighted, must furnish the means by which to navigate the world safely.

Descartes's blind man trips along the pages of the *Dioptrics*. Arrested by his cane, he stops . . . and grows perceptive. Is the light of the body, the light by which he perceives, the body's own or (like the eye's) a borrowed light? Does the body radiate or emit light, or does it merely receive it?

The question supposes that the body's light is like that of a visible object come to radiance. We need first understand the similitude. What happens when light lights on the body? The effect of light, of whatever nature, on a surface is twofold: both to reveal surface as surface and to cause it to give off light. This is nothing more than a restatement of Grosseteste's doctrine of multiplication: "A natural agent multiplies its power from itself to the recipient." The organic surface, when struck by light of a higher awareness, reveals its bidirectionality—automatism and consciousness, world-construct and "I"—inasmuch as it lightens up itself. The lightening up has nothing to do with visibility, clarity, intelligibility, or any other mark of sightedness. Instead, it concerns characteristics of body as body: density, consistency, weight, solidity, penetrability. The lighting of the body is "dark" because it has nothing to do with the light the sighted see. Yet its effect is not divorced from the visible. It is through lightening up of the body that invisibility becomes visible.

The texts of gravity and of brightness join in the body's lightening. A progressively melting organic strain—effortful as always—opens a progressively deepened state of presence. At each stage, less encumbrance stands in the way. At each stage, the body stands forth less masked by concerns projected by the intellectual frame. To lighten up, progressively and organically understood, is to be guided to states of fuller awareness. In each successive state, a circulation of percipient energy proper to the organism intensifies and deepens. When allowed to function unencumbered by external constraints, the body sloughs off a denial of its intrinsic lightness. That lightness, a feature of organic energy carried through specifically designed channels, contains a radiance. The awareness that melts weight and brings about lightness and radiance is proper to the body. It is the body's light, as distinct from the world's or the mind's.

An important shift takes place once the lightening up of the body is firmly established. Circulation twists back on itself, exhibiting the peculiar surface feature I have likened to a Möbius strip. Its twofoldness permits it to be related with a new awareness. The awareness, the source of the *lumen naturale*, is able to enter a receptive body and transform it into a radiant one. Sensitive and subtle, the body is ready to be inhabited. Once inhabited, the lightened body is not the encumbered organism set free, but one with new qualities and powers. It is the organism transformed from receptacle to radiant source.

The body, when lighted by a source energy in relation to its native percipience, is able to see, inside and out. A habitat for the former, it multiplies that energy's radiance by conjoining it to its own. By its twofold seeing, it negotiates the road to Dover and does not lose track of itself. It perceives through an enveloping awareness. To one who meets a body so lighted, it discloses itself as radiant, as emitting a visible radiation to the immediate environment. It is a body impressed with superabundant life—with a Life larger than life—that dwells within it.

How is the light of the body's light like that the sighted see? As in the *lumen naturale*, likeness is expressive of light. The fact of metaphor attests to similitude, and similitude, to the occurrence of light. Light *is* what is similar across shades of difference. Coloration, texture, shape, contour, purity, expansiveness, density, and brightness are different ways in which light—seen by the sighted or otherwise—marks its appearance. To read the text of similitude is to be light-sensitive, open to the presence of light, affected by light's qualities. Blinded and sighted share in that power.

The body's light and that by which the sighted see are species of light because they both are similars, not the other way around. The world is an interweaving of similars, strand placed on strand, layer on layer, until reality is thick with resemblance. Because of the "multiplication of species," one thing repeats another thing in its own way, according to its own particularity. Grosseteste makes note of the same phenomenon when he writes, "the agent sends the same power into sense and into matter, or into its own contrary, as heat sends the same thing into the sense of touch and into a cold body."[14] The result is a mirroring or echoing of aspects, a reiteration of one and the same in different contexts. Plants reflect human organs, birds' movements repeat human ones, the clouds copy the obscurities of the human heart, the winds blow like the vicissitudes of human fortune. The world presents itself face-to-face with our human face, so that to read features of the one is to know those of the other.

To see with the eyes or to perceive through the body's surface is to look onto an ambient field of resemblance and take notice of likeness. Such vision is necessarily hierarchical and hierophantic. Since correspondences exist between levels of reality, those who perceive deeper correspondences are thereby more fully endowed with reason. A rigorous training in attention is the entry fee to the program. Any philosophy articulating such a vision is necessarily elitist and antidemocratic. It divides humanity into those who have and those who have not. The light of similars reigns until vision is trained to object identification—through the insurrection Descartes helps engineer. Descartes holds object identification to be nonelitist, though this is not so. After Descartes, contraries or dissimilars take primacy. Vision shifts away from the light of similars, taking the more democratic form that showcases the ordinary visual object. The body's percipience as a mode of seeing is cast aside, its history revised, erased, and altogether annulled. Its coordinate, the ocean of similitude, is relegated to a kind of vague backdrop, a repository of resemblances that somehow allow one object to be known as *like* a second. The power of similars—to call elites into existence—is no longer a threat to the citizenry of perception. The world is made safe for democracy.

8

The Sight of the Blind

Light and Action

Flashes of light that momentarily brighten some corner of the intellectual frame—the *lumen naturale*—hold great attraction for thinkers of a reformist disposition. Descartes seizes on the bright, democratizing potential. Coming from nature, it is a design feature of our mental apparatus. Since no special training is required to master its illumination, it belongs to all, philosopher-priest and commoner alike. It is, therefore, unlikely to be co-opted by an elite. True, while there are, as Descartes acknowledges in the *Regulae*, "far more of such truths than most people observe," a change in attitude would suffice to make us less disdainful and more appreciative of them. To favor the self-evidence of truth in general is to support democratizing movements throughout the philosophical realm because they permit no person justifiably to claim privilege in the field of knowledge. An attitude change with respect to the *lumen naturale*, therefore, is an appropriate demand for a democratic revolutionary.

A real shortcoming of the program stems from revolutionary blindness. Enthusiasm dominates where reflection should. Descartes picks up a weapon—"a conception formed by unclouded mental attention, so easy and distinct as to leave no room for doubt"—without taking a closer look at its attachments. A good rule of thumb is that all that glitters is not good. With the *lumen naturale*, this is especially true. At one point, Descartes asserts that "we shall learn how to employ our mental intuition from comparing it with the way in which we employ our eyes."[1] The Cartesian embrace of the light of nature ultimately leads to a paralysis of the forces of action more potent than a stroke. Descartes perpetuates a long tradition's refusal to act.

That refusal is born in looking askance at the action of light. The fruit of the *lumen natural's* action—a clear concept, idea, thought-con-

119

struct—is prized above all others. Like manna it can feed a democratic body politic hungry for knowledge. But light's action itself? A lacuna in thought concerning the light of reason reveals more of tradition's grasp on Descartes. The light the sighted see is invisible in action. A beam of light in a dark room is seen through the dance of dust motes. Take them away and (as in a vacuum or in outer space) the beam disappears! The eye sees, not light's action, but the action's results. We see things by how light affects them, by how they absorb and reflect light. Radiating or unreflected light we the sighted do not see. It is the very invisibility of action that bedevils the Cartesian project.

The concealment is apparent in unvoiced questions. On what does an "unclouded mental attention" act? From where does its action proceed? What part does a person play in the epistemic drama? Descartes fails to behold that the *lumen naturale* places him squarely within the domain of the blind. The stop is at work. It brings an end to unchecked habits of mental association and frees a quality of attentiveness. It discloses how customary ideas and mental patterns conceal an opening to deep thought. It allows a space in the intellectual clutter for an unconditioned, unpremeditated response. What is similar makes its appearance, manifesting itself in its clear and distinctive lighting. It is apprehended by the intellect within its frame. The *lumen naturale* is the energy of the stop, reflected back to mental attention.

Light becomes visible upon reflection, or, in Grosseteste's descriptive phrase, in the multiplication of species. When we look at reflection in the case of the sighted, a certain portion of light is absorbed by the body on which it falls. The same holds true for the *lumen naturale*. It is precisely the study from which Descartes turns back. Light reflected back to mind has a destination other than mind. It is light absorbed by the organism. It is the advent of the stop.

The light of reason is none other than the stop, reflected into and constrained by the intellectual frame. Ease of mind and distinctness of thought are aspects of a poised moment. Had Descartes not turned from them, they would be adequate civic virtues for a democratic body. They would have permitted citizens' responses in just measure to their intellectual analyses. Mind, no longer beset by a dim, cramped space where depth is hidden by surface, would allow thought to express itself. A citizenry, furthermore, would have been able to eschew isolation and embrace community. For the stop arrests an attitude of control, driven by a fear of and vulnerability to the dark unknown. It dissolves a need to foreknow, presuppose, prefigure, and plan out in advance, just as it dissolves the need to arm, fortify, and consolidate territory. A deeper exigence of present experience regains supremacy. Had Descartes been steadfast, a democratic impulse would have brought forth greatness. In the moment of the stop, the *lumen naturale* appears and seems to outshine—like the sun the stars—all elitist figments and all separatist icons.

Descartes shrinks from a more wholehearted embrace of the huddled figure of the blind man. Is he merely squeamish? In fact, the reason goes deeper. Descartes plays the role without feeling it. As a result, his confrontation with that which the blind dwell in—darkness—arouses an archaic fear. It blunts his ambition to topple philosophical elites, especially the edifice of sightedness. He turns back from the organic milieu, recently discovered through the stop, toward a backlit intellectual frame. When the *lumen naturale* gleams in darkness, he clutches it as protection from his agony. Intellection provides an amulet against solitude of novelty.

Against a monster of despair, there is no protection—unless desensitization is protective. Unless one threads the dark labyrinth and confronts the Minotaur, no transformation of self-doubt is possible. To follow the percipient energy's descent through intellect leads to a discovery different from a new idea. The energy is destined to meet the organism. Felt by the body, the stop differs markedly from that felt by the mind. The full stop occurs at the physical center. It occupies the whole person. A surface specifically endowed with perceptive qualities appears. Concentration—not merely mental attention—gathers poised before the moment. The gathering is not idle. It is a gathering of concentration for the purposes of action.

Therein lies the greatest secret of the stop. Intellect's light sees but is powerless to do. The body's light sees and is able to do.

Samson is chained, each massive arm to a marble pillar. Revenge has brought him here, among the host of his enemy. It drives him toward fulfillment of a violent deed. His blindness teaches a preparation so that action does not misplay. An ingathering and focus of attention neutralizes the associative functioning of mind and places all available energy at the disposal of his purpose. Because the whole person is addressed, Samson's effort to act takes on another quality. It incorporates the stop.

Samson is blind. His blindness guides him to the brute fact of effort. Effort is needed for the act of perception that we the sighted enact effortlessly. Having sensed a resisting world, he can move with assurance. Though this is sufficient for him, it is hardly his sole reward. "The initial judgment of existence," Maine de Biran reminds us,

> comes from apperception of effort which in the same intu-
> ition constitutes the subject of effort and the alien terminus
> which exists solely as the force of resistance; through it . . .
> the myself becomes capable of knowing its own limits and
> of circumscribing them.[2]

Usually, resistance consumes Samson. He loses himself in reaction to it. This occasion is different. In the moment when Samson engages the effort, he meets not only what opposes the intended act, but its author—himself. Remembering himself, he again faces in two directions. Before him lies the world of form; behind, the world of formlessness. The one draws him into abstraction, the other, into absorption. In the moment of effort, however, it is different. Neither's claim is overreaching. Samson is free.

Furthermore, his purpose meets the act intended by it because his action is in harmony with the times. Only when he is organically in contact with himself is Samson able to act in accordance with the times. His custom has been otherwise—to force his act upon an unwilling world, to not flinch when thwarted. His is not an unthinking reflex, but the opposite. Once he decides to act, his impulse is seized by his intellectual frame and analyzed, criticized, and evaluated. Diversion disrupts an awareness of resistance, thereby breaking an easy connection with agency. When awareness is absent and the predetermined time to act arises, brute strength is his lever by which to impose his will. He finds the world unreceptive to his decision regarding the time and manner of action. His results are counterproductive, even contrary to his intention.

Related to himself, Samson's position is radically different. Agency is inextricably linked with timing. The "I can" has at its disposal an acute sensitivity to tempo, pulse, and beat, since it is through the dimension of timing that Samson meshes with the world's events. It is the peculiar surface of perception that interfaces agent and patient, active and receptive. The text of communication is written in the timing dimension, for through it organic percipience "sees."

Percipience is of the rhythmic language of unfolding events. Far from being a secondary property, the vibrational aspect of occurrences is primary when perception is geared to action. Neglect of it in favor of more-intellectual frames is the main cause of the tradition's paralysis on the brink of action. Because of it, gears of action do not mesh intention with an intelligence meant to direct them. Devotion to conceptual control of situations blocks a direct route and mandates that intention be actualized indirectly—through daydream and compulsive behavior. Samson's secret is to reject a mental attention (a *lumen natural*) and cultivate a wider, deeper, more organic attentiveness. That secret safeguards him from falling into the Hamlet role.

Like a dancer, gymnast, or athlete, Samson does not think about his perception before acting. When it is time for action, Samson perceives it through a "feel" in his body. The mental events that accompany perception do not distract him. He remains available to the dictates of his time.

An Embodied Sight for the Sighted

Descartes's secret hope is to install the hegemony of the blind. Their empowerment would expiate the millenia of their repression. It would also atone for the elitism of the sighted, who would become the newly downtrodden. But Descartes's motivation overdetermines the desired results. Revenge, resentment, and other reactive emotions demand a logic of exclusion. His grand project fails. We, however, need not be so defeated. It is possible to ask after a reconciliation of sight and blindness. Can the sighted learn to see as the blind do? Can vision be informed by a consciousness greater than the intellect?

Initially, I want to take the unusual step of asking the inverse question: Can the blind learn to see like the sighted? Rather than repeat Molyneux's query, discussed above in the form that Locke gives it, I am more interested in what the empirical data show. Three centuries after Descartes's *Dioptrics*, the surgeons Moreau and LePrince operated on an eight-year-old who had been congenitally blind. The operation was successful from a surgical point of view. Both eyes were made fully functional when the cataracts were removed. When the bandages were off, Moreau moved his hand across the boy's field of vision. When asked what he saw, he said, "I don't know." When asked whether he saw movement, he said, "I don't know." Only when allowed to touch the moving hand did he exclaim, "It's moving!"

Moreau concluded that functionally intact eyes are a necessary but not a sufficient cause of sight. "It would be an error to suppose," he writes

> that a patient whose sight has been restored to him by surgical intervention can thereafter see the external world. The eyes have certainly obtained the power to see, but the employment of this power, which as a whole constitutes the act of seeing, still has to be acquired from the very beginning. The operation itself has no more value than that of preparing the eyes to see; education is the most important fact. . . . To give back sight to a congenitally blind person is more the work of an educator than of a surgeon.[3]

The result is corroborated by Gregory and Wallace. They studied the case of a fifty-year-old man, blind from ten months old, who received corneal transplants. The operation gave him complete functional use of his eyes. His first visual experience was the face of the surgeon, which was a "blur." Only by inference (having heard a voice and knowing the location of the surgeon) did identification by vision take place. There followed a slow, painful process of learning to see. Most often, the man had to touch an object with his hands in order to begin to see it by sight. Learning the correlation was a matter of effort expended at great personal cost.

Studies with other cases of blind patients reveal a startlingly similar pattern.[4] Most feel threatened by new sighted impressions and seek the security and reliability of old, blind ones. Sightedness is to be gained only through bitter struggle. Many tragically turn from the world of the sighted, to self-imposed, hysterical blindness or to death. These are observations not contained in Molyneux's problem. We, furthermore, can learn by looking at an exception to the rule. Anna Mae Pennica underwent a cataract operation at age sixty-two after having been blind from birth.[5] So far, the story follows that of many other cataract cases. Anna Mae's eyes were restored to complete functionality. Rather than experiencing a paralytic disruption in her world, Anna Mae saw immediately. Her report was that the world is "just about as I imagined it would be."

Stronger confirmation of her visual perception came from her correctly identifying colors and from being able to read and write. There was none of the usual postoperative trauma. What accounts for Anna Mae's exceptional response? In her childhood, her mother guided her hand in "making our letters" on a blackboard. Spelling and writing followed a similar and rigorous training method. Her mother instilled a confidence in her by saying, "When you learn to see, you will be able to read and write." In Anna Mae's case, her body was called into play. Her experience of visual objects, unlike that of other patients, was not restricted to mental associations occasioned by impressions from other senses. Muscular movement initiated under her mother's guidance involved effort. With effort came the stop. The stop defined both a resistance to and an agent of the movement. It also provided an organic impression correlate to the contour of the glyph or the traced visual form. The soma was called to participate in the act of perception. The rudiments of sight were taken into the body. When conditions were ripe, Anna Mae was able to see.

Thus can the blind, against all odds, learn to see like the sighted. If their "education," to use Moreau's term, centers on attending to the body's response to what the sighted see in a visual impression, we can be hopeful. Such training is highly demanding, with a time premium on it. Anna Mae succeeded where others failed because her attention was properly focused at the appropriate time in her life. Returned to the organic milieu, it developed into an awareness of how the body itself effortfully responds to a realm that the sighted perceive without effort. What Lusseyran discovered by himself, Anna Mae found through instruction.

What about the reverse training: Can the sighted learn to perceive like the blind—without having to go blind? I want to understand a way for the sighted to return to a sightedness of the fully embodied person. Are the two cases—the blind learning sightedness and the sighted learning to see as the blind—parallel? They seem to be. First, they agree in method and aim. Both incorporate a very stringent demand on the attention: to be stopped and to return to the organic fold. Both training regimes are framed for the gifted and exceptional. Second, both are remedial. The one obviously is to restore the visual function to the blind handicapped by its absence. The other is to remedy the habituated interference of intellect in the act of visually seeing. It is to return the visual function to its full potential for those handicapped by a lack of clear-sightedness.

To bring either the blind or the sighted to see involves a reharmonization of functional aspects of person, intellect, feeling, and body. Inharmonious functioning is manifested noticeably in the predominance of intellect in experience. We see with our brains rather than our eyes. To allow harmony to reign over our different aspects requires a cultivation of the stop. The stop contains a specific that, acting on awareness and organism alike, opens one to the source of lighting. That lighting Descartes intuited, and, I have argued, it is obscured by a tradition of spiritual elitism that sanctions intellect's appropriation of perception—that is, that legitimates a dysfunctional mode of perceiving. Since Descartes's bungled job of exposing the bias and exploding the tradition, a double task remains. Both the untampered tradition *and* Descartes's botched revision must be repaired. A job half-done is worse than one not done at all.

In the moment of the stop, the obscuration itself is lit up by background lighting. Its effect—nondisclosure—is cast aside. Related to one another, organism and awareness share a common source. Each is like the other in that, being similars, both are lighted from above. A hidden relation of the two reveals the source of the similitude: a higher, more inclusive level of energy. It is precisely this specific that Descartes leaves out of his account. Like Hamlet, a spirit of revenge prevents him from serving a higher purpose. Trapped in his ego, cut off from the percipience that informs agency of timing, he remains unavailable to the moment of action. Lacking percipience, Descartes lacks the lighting by which ego grows transparent. His entire project defines and is defined by ego's bounds.

To train the sighted to see with their bodies' eyes, not with their brains, is to urge on them the cultivation of the stop. When automatism comes to a stop, the action of percipient energy is felt. An organic awareness sloughs off the influence of the conceptual field and opens to a new influence. The eyes (and other senses) function unimpeded by intellectual expectations. The world they behold belongs to a wider cosmos. What is seen then signifies the wider cosmos as it expresses itself through the visual field. Visual objects possess an aura of meaning derived from the higher realm. They are not understood as objects of pleasure, convenience, or utility inasmuch as they do not wholly belong to the world of such valuations. They are objects of sacred interest.

The eyes of an embodied look behold a realm of visible signs where we are accustomed to see mere objects. Such eyes see things other than foci of possible objectifying appearance. They read the signature of deep meaning. Things seen thus point to a level of reality hidden by the reduction of meaning from triad to dyad. A door to the forgotten level opens through the stop. The stop brings relation with it. Through relation, the gulf between sign and signified is bridged. A deep significance of the things we encounter grows visible to the eyes. When the visible world serves something in addition to our private purposes, that service is primary. The world the sighted see ceases to be an opaque reflection of private values and instead grows transparent with higher purpose. Through our interaction with its everyday things, a feeling of participation in deep meaning arises. Returning to home in the body, we are returned to our place in an order of things, ever new, ever regenerating.

9

The Story of Oedipus

> What! Light should only exist inasmuch as
> it is seen? No! *You* would not exist if the
> light did not see *you*!
> —Goethe

The Crossroads

The story of Oedipus begins at the crossroads. It is not the first incident in time, but the origin of all action, before and after. With Oepidus's story is the beginning of a major stream of our tradition, the Hellenistic. It is no accident that two blinded heroes of gigantic stature, Oedipus and Samson, representing the Hellenistic and Hebraic, respectively, stand as twin columns on the monument of our nativity. They are icons of warning.

It is said that

There were three highways
Coming together at a place I passed.[1]

So Sophocles describes the scene in the midst of which Oedipus arrives in haste toward a self-imposed exile. By name, it is Phokis, where the Theban Way divides into roads toward Delphi and Daulia. The oracle at Delphi earlier had spoken of Oedipus's being his father's murderer. It had marked him as revolutionary, an overthrower of tradition. In Corinth, where Paul at a later time would write letters speaking of another revolutionary, Jesus, Oedipus grew up. Polybos was the name of the man he took to be his father, and loved. The news at Delphi struck terror in his heart. He forthwith resolved to flee his native land to avoid being an accomplice to a fate he disdained. His way to the

129

crossroads was, contrary to that of Homer's hero Odysseus, a flight
from a house where he lived. The crossroads, the first place Oedipus
comes to, measures the great distance traveled from home. In all his
travels, Odysseus never comes to a crossroads.

Though he was educated as a king's son, Oedipus is unprepared
for the crossroads. Avoidance preoccupies him. Told of his time, he is
intent on refusal. His sight is narrowed in the bitterness of this attitude.
He has mapped out a plan, to seek "a land where I should never see the
evil/Sung by the oracle." The thought obsesses him. It drives him
onward so that he goes without seeing. He does not see that he is cut
off from himself.

At the crossroads, he comes under attack. "The groom leading the
horses" forces him off the road. It is a boy, not yet old enough to wield
a weapon, but rage flares up in Oedipus. What springs from him is not
instinct (since that remains hidden, unheeded) but an ordeal of intellect. It is the reaction, not of an animal, but of a man thwarted in purpose. Much later, as an old man at Colonus, he will claim his innocence,
saying he acted involuntarily. If the voluntary requires a mind free from
preoccupation, Oedipus is correct. He is unable to act voluntarily
because he cannot see what faces him. He is at a crossroads. There is a
choice. The choice is depends on stopping to read the signs.

For Oedipus there is no stop. After the groom, the young chario-
teer comes after him. The first shadow of a beard darkens his cheeks.
From childhood, he has been in the service of the king. Now at last, like
his father before him, he has been entrusted with the horses' reins.
Unlike Phaeton, who took on his father Helios's chariot too early, he
shows no weak will. He has kept the horses under control and now will
allow no common brigand to threaten his master. When the boy-groom
is turned aside, he plunges the chariot straight for Oedipus. The blow
from Oedipus's club knocks him lifeless to the gutter.

There is only the old man left. His gray hair tousled by wind, his
purple cloak loose around his neck, the man has a fierce pride burning
in his eyes. It shows strength far out of proportion to the shrunken
body. More than anything else, the eyes goad Oedipus into action. For
a split second, they penetrate Oedipus' armor and hold him motionless
by the roadside. They question, not by interrogation, but gently,
searchingly, like a father's eyes. A terror rises in him. It catapults him
into action. The heavy club describes an arc in the bright air. At its
zenith, the old man with his double goad a horse-length away, a flicker
of recognition passes over his eyes. It is mirrored by an expression—

almost familiar—on the other's face. Then the club descends. Then there is death.

Oedipus does not pause to examine his victims. "I killed him/I killed them all," he says. More enemies may be near. Above, vultures are already circling. The crossroads is a place of danger, and of possibility. The possibility is of an encounter. The danger is of refusal. The encounter is with himself. It is refused.

The Blinding

Oedipus's history, which is ours, begins with blind refusal. He has eyes only for what furthers or impedes flight. Revenge speaks through him. When describing how Laios, king of Thebes and his father, approached him, Oedipus proclaims, "He was paid back, and more!" Revenge prepares him for combat and drives him over the brink without pause. He is the servant of revenge. His master bids him to grip a club and swing.

Revenge has prepared an intellectual frame for his prison. In it, it turns Oedipus round, facing away. It has instrumented him well and made him skillful at riddles and state management. Temples, city walls, highways, trade, the accumulation of wealth, the waging of war: he throws himself into frenzied activity. Thebes's luster grows. It palliates Oedipus's inner life. There, a primal terror in moments rises in his gorge. Always, the shadow of weakness passes but leaves great weariness in its wake. Only the magnificence of his will allows him to endure.

Then he is tested. A plague devastates the city. Measures are tried by priest and physician but to no avail. What is disease but a disequilibrium of vital forces, a preoccupation of thought and feeling that impedes a circulation of vivifying energies? Cure always follows the law of similars. What cures is the same as what causes illness in a healthy being. But first, the illness must be perceived. Signs must be read.

Teiresias is brought in. Blind, he has a gift of second sight. He is able to see what is hidden, to divine what is to be. His percipience is mocked by Oedipus but Teiresias resists involvement. The mocking continues. Finally, he sends forth a sharp probe, saying, "You, with both your eyes, are blind." Oedipus is again set before the crossroads. The earlier scene passes like the shred of a dream. Who had once stood there? Teiresias speaks again:

> You do not even know the blind wrongs
> That you have done on earth and in the world below.

Oedipus in his terror grows subdued. A new struggle in him replaces that which raged outside him. He feels himself resist the mechanism of his sight and pull back into a forgotten fold. The crossroads calls for understanding. His response is to recognize a new impulse.

Effort does not persist. The next moment finds him bent on world making, defiant and dismissive. This is the one who met Laios the king at the crossroads and slew him. Teiresias sees and prophesies:

> A blind man
> Who has his eyes now; a penniless man who is rich now;
> And he will go tapping the strange earth with his staff.

The prophecy names the cure. Blindness in the healthy and sighted causes disease, while in those with impaired sight it cures a condition of pathology. What the disease is called matters little. Plague, revenge, intellectualism: in terms of the action of cure, it is the opaque organic center that is addressed, that which bears no description.

The remainder of the story tells how Oedipus's refusal melts. Slowly the body remembers. It stops thought. There is the scar at the ankles that corresponds to abandonment in infancy. It has not forgotten how his father had him bound and his mother had him left for the beasts of the mountain. Slowly the stop works its action. He reinhabits the body he had deserted, repeating the desertion of it by his parents. Through the body circulates a new awareness, a percipience of things about him, of himself. Slowly he works his way back to the crossroads.

Oedipus walks along the Theban Way. Just as he comes to the place where three roads meet, one from Delphi (whence he comes), one from Daulia, and one from Thebes (whence he goes), a chariot comes from the other way. It and its party bear down on him, a single man. He is again at the crossroads. He recognizes his reaction to the ensemble, and that stops him. His aggressive impulse remains in question as he tries to read the situation. For a moment, he does not repeat his evasions. He does nothing. He awaits the sign.

> O three roads, dark ravine, woodland and way
> Where three roads met.

The cure, which is to save Thebes from pestilence, must be administerd by Oedipus's own hands. This would not be possible if it were an act of revenge. It is a new blindness to end the old blindness

that Teiresias prescribed. It is not punishment for his crime, the parri-
cide, unless cure is punishment for the disease's victim. Proof of cure
comes from Oedipus's own revelation: "Death will not ever come to me
through sickness/Or in any natural way."

Oedipus's history is a tragic one. The crossroads is the place of
tragedy. The tragedy, one of timing, is not Oedipus's self-blinding, since
that brings the plague to an end and ends well for the multitude. The
history is a tragic one because the cure comes too late. Damage has
already been done, for which there can be no atonement.

Redrawing the Crossroads

The history of avoiding what preoccupies the attention begins with
Oedipus at the crossroads. That history is being written even up until
now. An end of history and of tragedy involves a return to the crossroads. Oedipus stops and ceases to give attention to flight. It is a
moment of recognition. Oedipus recognizes the unavoidability of the
situation.

There is the Delphic oracle and all it has said. The image has been
branded in his mind. It directs his escape. And there is the encounter
at the crossroads, the cloud of dust rising from the other road, and the
party of five racing headlong to meet him. Blood rises in him as it has
each time he has come to the crossroads. His grip closes on the handle
of the massive club. His breath grows shallow as his muscles clench.

There are several variations of what ensues.

Even as his heart pounds, a mood of inexplicable familiarity
passes over him. The club in his right hand has a strange feel to it,
though he has carried its weight since leaving Delphi. Exertions of the
past days drop away from him. The elation at coming to the Theban
Way has passed from dismay at the new challenge to a sense of uncan-
niness. While the royal escort bears down on him, Oedipus is partly
abstracted. It is as he were in a place he had been in before. When? Was
it a dream of portent? Was it in the innocence of childhood, when
impressions are set with magical powers? Or does the mood itself
bespeak the presence of a sign?

Slowly, as though emerging from another element, Oedipus gathers himself. It will be a battle to the death. Suddenly his ancient fear falls

into place, and with it, his ire. The club is raised above the sun. Its first victim is about to fall.

Oedipus stands on a low knoll just west of where the three roads come together. It commands a view of a narrow plain. Exhausted from flight, he experiences none of the relief he had anticipated. Corinth and a dreaded past lie many days behind, yet the words of the Pythoness of Delphi echo all the more loudly here. A sudden weakness frightens him. When he looks up, the cloud of an enemy speeds toward him along the highway. He steels himself and girds his loins for battle.

A shadow passes over his face. A hawk or great desert bird momentarily eclipses the sun. Oedipus looks back over his shoulder in the direction he has come. Has he done the right thing? The question dissolves the moment he grips his war club. When he looks south again, his jaw is set, eyes glaring.

At the crossroads is a well. An oily, dark liquid comes up in Oedipus's hand as he scoops to drink. On its surface, he sees reflected a face he does not recognize. Could the ardors of the journey have aged him so greatly? When he looks again, he sees the face of his father.

Oedipus experiences vertigo when he stands. The face was not Polybus's, yet he does not know what name to attach to the new knowledge. From a distance, the royal party races toward the crossroads. Oedipus does not understood the languor of his limbs nor his composed mind, but as the chariot nears him, the old man is the one whose face he saw a moment before in the image. Though the groom is menacing, Oedipus allows the chariot to pass by him. For an instant, the old man's eyes meet his. Oedipus has the sense of being recognized.

Oedipus is at the crossroads. He has camped there for several days, awaiting an augury. Waiting has not been easy. He has poured libations and listened to the birds' cries, but to no avail. Despair wells up in him. He knows that to go boldly forth without confirmation would be impiety. He is at an impasse.

Suddenly a plume of dust catches the light of the morning sun. Someone approaches along the road to the south. Oedipus peers attentively out from under a flap of his tabernacle. The question of his flight becomes apparent. Why has he been called to this place? A sense of a secret purposes envelops him as he comes out to greet the strangers. A club by his side, he is armed but more intent on responding appropriately. The chariot passes by. He and the king exchange glances. Oedipus breaks camp and takes the road to Daulia.

There is the stop.

In light of its percipience, automatic reaction momentarily ceases. Body and intellect come into relation and, through that relation, become related to a higher purpose. Flight from fate meets fate actualized in the fire of recognition. One is superimposed on the other with nothing left over. Oedipus finds his place with time to behold it. The assumption of the tragic crossroads is that one always escapes the unavoidable—until it is too late. A history of avoidance ends with recognition of time.

Tragedy assumes the unavoidability of unconsciousness. A fate has been ordained for Oedipus; he can do nothing, therefore, but fulfill it. The "flaw" of his, and our, humanity turns on the lack of awareness. His action must endlessly repeat this flaw. Tragedy does not take into account the stop.

The stop is necessity of action brought to the power of light. It is necessity made luminous, transparent and transformed. It is an uncanny force. It is of at least equal magnitude to the fate decreed by oracles and divined by seers. It introduces a power of mystery into the equation of action. The result might be fated or it might sidestep fate by way of individual choice. The result might be a surprise.

When Oedipus begins to wield the stop instead of his club, the fact of avoidability is irrevocably altered. Flight arrested, preoccupation suspended, vision cleared, he faces his life differently. Percipience brings knowledge of the dimension of timing. No longer does he strain to fend off his past. His hand unclenches, his huge biceps relax. He watches himself go forth to meet what has been pursuing him.

In that battle, Oedipus goes forth as a human. He sees with his own eyes, the eyes of his own flesh, and sees the matter of choice. To react is to be beaten by an outcome already decreed. To act under the power of percipient light, the power of mystery, is to greet an unknown outcome. In it, defeat remains possible. But so long as the mechanism of preoccupation and presumption is arrested, Oedipus places himself under a different set of laws. In that moment, he is free.

As the chariot pulls up, Oedipus, the man, faces two directions. One is the set of habits and tendencies, inherited and acquired. The other is a cluster of impulses, equal in power to the first, unknown in outcome. One leads with certainty to a tragic end. The other is unwalked and with an uncertain destination. One is fear and security (they are the same); the other is hope and caring. To face the two directions, Oedipus must remain on the edge of things. The moment he moves, he falls without love into his fate. It waits for him, maw gaping, a monster ready to devour . . . or be tamed.

Notes

1. Blindness and Light

1. Descartes, *Meditations*, Meditation 1, in *Philosophical Writings*, ed. Elizabeth Anscombe and Peter Geach.

2. Descartes, *Rules for the Direction of the Mind*, Rule 3, in *Philosophical Writings*, p. 153.

3. Descartes, *The Dioptrics*, in *Philosophical Writings*, p. 244.

4. Descartes, *The Dioptrics*, p. 246.

5. Ibid., p. 247.

6. Ibid., p. 248.

7. Descartes, *The Dioptrics*, p. 241.

8. Descartes, *The Dioptrics*, p. 241.

9. Ibid.

10. Descartes, *The Principles of Philosophy*, Part 4, in *Philosophical Writings*, p. 236.

11. Berkeley, *A New Theory of Vision*, p. 30.

12. Ibid., p. 63.

2. The Ceaseless Agony of the Blind

1. Milton, *Samson Agonistes*, in *The English Poems of John Milton*. All citations in the text are to this edition.

2. Descartes, *The Principles of Philosophy*, 2. 4, p. 199.

3. Ibid., 2. 8, p. 201.

4. Descartes, *The Dioptrics*, pp. 248–49.

5. Descartes, *The Principles of Philosophy*, 1. 78, p. 198.

6. Ibid., 1. 71, p. 196.

7. Leonardo, cited in Vassily Zubov, *Leonardo da Vinci* (Cambridge, Mass. 1968), pp. 131ff.

8. Roger Bacon, *Part of the Opus tertium of Roger Bacon, Including a Fragment Now Printed for the First Time*, ed. A. G. Little (Aberdeen, 1912).

9. Al-kindi, *De aspectibus*, prop. 7; cited in David Lindberg, *Theories of Vision from Al-Kindi to Kepler* (Chicago: University of Chicago Press, 1976), p. 22.

10. Morris R. Cohen and I. E. Drabkin, tr., *A Sourcebook on Greek Science* (Cambridge, Mass., 1958), p. 257.

11. A. C. Crombie, *Robert Grosseteste and the Origins of Experimental Science 1100–1700* (Oxford, 1953), p. 96.

3. The Vanishing Eye

1. Leon Battist Alberti, *On Painting and on Sculpture: The Latin Texts of De Pictura and De Statua, Edited with English Translations, Introduction, and Notes*, tr. Cecil Grayson. (London, 1972), p. 54.

2. Ibid., p. 48.

3. Ibid., pp. 68–69.

4. Ibid.

5. Leonardo da Vinci, *On Painting,* p. 33.

6. Descartes, *Meditations,* p. 75.

7. Descartes, *The Dioptrics,* pp. 245–46.

8. Locke, *An Essay Concerning Human Understanding,* pp. 75–76.

9. Ibid.

4. Blindness and the Sign

1. Paracelsus, *Selected Writings,* p. 120. All page number citations in the text are to this edition.

2. C. S. Peirce, *The Philosophical Writings of Peirce.* All citations of page numbers are to this volume.

3. Descartes, *Rules,* Rule 12, p. 170.

4. Cited in Norman Kemp Smith, *New Studies in the Philosophy of Descartes,* p. 33.

5. Ibid. p 35.

6. Ibid. p. 36.

7. Ibid., p. 37.

8. Ibid., p. 39.

9. Descartes, *Rules,* p. 155.

10. Ibid.

5. The Organism of Text

1. Paracelsus, cited in Walter Pagel, *Paracelsus,* pp. 78–79.

2. *I Ching,* p. 171.

6. Sight and Movement

1. Maine de Biran, *Habitude*, in *L'effort*, pp. 58–59; my translations here and in what follows.

2. Maine de Biran, *Faits psychologiques et physiologiques*, in *L'effort*, p. 43.

3. Ibid., p. 44.

4. Ibid., p. 45.

5. Ibid.

6. Maine de Biran, *Aperception immediate*, in *L'effort*, p. 23.

7. Lusseyran, *And There Was Light*, p. 14.

8. Ibid., p. 16.

9. Ibid., p. 17.

10. Ibid., p. 18.

11. Lusseyran, *The Blind in Society and Blindness*, p. 31.

7. The Light of the Stop

1. Descartes, *Meditations*, III, p. 79.

2. Descartes, *Rules*, Rule 3, p. 155.

3. Ibid.

4. Ibid., Rule 12, p. 169.

5. Ibid.

6. Descartes, *Meditations*, II, p. 73.

7. Augustine, *De trinitate*, p. 164.

8. Bacon, *The Opus Majus of Roger Bacon*, 1: 216.

9. Plato, *Republic*, tr. Paul Shorey, in *The Collected Dialogues of Plato*, ed. Edith Hamilton and Huntington Cairns (Princeton: Princeton University Press, 1961), 7. 517c.

10. Grosseteste, cited in, Edward Grant, ed., *A Sourcebook in Medieval Science* (Cambridge, Mass., 1974), p. 385.

11. Descartes, *Meditations,* III, p. 82.

12. Ibid.

13. Grosseteste, cited in Crombie, *Robert Grosseteste*, p. 110.

14. Grosseteste, cited in Grant, *A Sourcebook in Medieval Science*, p. 385.

8. The Sight of the Blind

1. Descartes, *Rules,* Rule 9, p. 28.

2. Maine de Biran, *Memoire* IV.2, in *Oeuvres de Maine de Biran*, ed. P. Tisserand (Paris, 1920–29; cited in Paul Ricoeur, *Freedom and Nature*, tr. Erazim Kohak (Evanston, Ill., 1966), p. 334.

3. Cited in M. von Senden, *Space and Sight,* p. 160.

4. See *ibid.*

5. Described in Pettit, "Report on Anna Mae Pennica."

9. The Story of Oedipus

1. Citations regarding the story of Oedipus are from, Sophocles, *The Oedipus Cycle.*

Bibliography

Alberti, Leon Battista. *On Painting*. Translated by John R. Spencer. New Haven, 1966.

Augustine. *De trinitate*. Translated by Marcus Dods and Arthur W. Haddan. In *A Select Library of the Nicene and Post-Nicene Fathers of the Christian Church*. Vol. 3. Edited by Philip Schaff. Buffalo, 1887.

Bacon, Roger. *The Opus Majus of Roger Bacon*. Translated by Robert B. Burke. Philadelphia, 1928. Reprint New York, 1962.

Berkeley, George. *A New Theory of Vision*. London: Dent, 1910.

Descartes, René. *Discourse on Method, Optics, Geometry, and Meteorology*. Translated by Paul J. Olscamp. New York: Bobbs-Merrill, 1965.

————. *The Philosophical Works of Descartes*. Translated by Elizabeth Haldane and G. R. T. Ross. Cambridge: Cambridge University Press, 1911.

————. *Philosophical Writings*. Edited by Elizabeth Anscombe and Peter Geach, London: Nelson, 1964.

Edgerton, Samuel Y., Jr. *The Renaissance Rediscovery of Linear Perspective* New York: Basic Books, 1975.

Foucault, Michel. *The Order of Things*. New York: Random House, 1970.

Grosseteste, Robert. *On Light*. Translated by Clare C. Riedl. Milwaukee, 1942.

I Ching. Translated by Richard Wilhelm. Princeton: Princeton University Press, 1950.

Leonardo da Vinci. *The Notebooks of Leonardo da Vinci*. Translated by Edward MacCurdy. New York, 1939.

———. *On Painting: A Lost Book*. Edited and translated by Carlo Pedretti. Berkeley, 1964.

Lindberg, David C. *Theories of Vision from Al-Kindi to Kepler*. Chicago: University of Chicago Press, 1976.

Locke, John. *An Essay Concerning Human Understanding*. Edited by A.S. Pringle-Pattison. Oxford: Clarendon Press, 1924.

Lusseyran, Jacques. *The Blind in Society and Blindness: A New Seeing of the World*. New York: Myrin Institute, 1973.

———. *And There Was Light*. Translated by Elizabeth R. Cameron. New York: Parabola, 1987.

Maine de Biran. *L'effort*. Edited by A. Drevet. Paris: Presses Universitaires de France, 1966

Marcel, Gabriel. *Being and Having*. Translated by Katherine Farrer. New York: Harper & Row, 1965.

Milton, John. *Samson Agonistes*. In *The English Poems of John Milton*. London: Oxford University Press, 1936.

Pagel, Walter. *Paracelsus*. New York: S. Karger, 1958.

Paracelsus. *Selected Writings*. Edited by Jolande Jacobi. Princeton: Princeton University Press, 1979.

Peirce, C. S. *The Philosophical Writings of Peirce*. Edited by Justus Buchler. New York: Dover, 1940.

Pettit, Thomas. "Report on Anna Mae Pennica." Jules Stein Eye Institute, UCLA, Los Angeles. *Brain/Mind Bulletin 6*.

Sebba, Gregor. *The Dream of Descartes*. Carbondale, Ill.: Southern Illinois University Press, 1987.

Smith, Norman Kemp. *New Studies in the Philosophy of Descartes.* New York: Russell & Russell, 1963.

Sophocles. *The Oedipus Cycle.* Translated by Dudley Fitts and Robert Fitzgerald. New York: Harcourt, Brace, 1949.

von Senden, M. *Space and Sight: The Perception of Space and Shape in the Congenitally Blind before and after Operation.* Translated by Peter Heath. Glencoe, Ill.: Free Press, 1960.

White, John. *The Birth and Rebirth of Pictorial Space.* Cambridge: Harvard University Press, 1987.

Index

Action: and choice, 16; concentration of form before, 37; conceptualizing, 24; deferred, 34; destructive, 27; at a distance, 3; double, 5, 6; field of, 35; form before, 29; and indifference, 40; interstices of, xi; of light, 113; movement toward, viii; necessity of, 135; origin of, 129; perception geared to, 122; and poise, 14; purposes of, 121; and reading, 74; relinquishing, 4; repetitive, 4; self-aware, 14; through contact, 3; unity of, 108; unpoised, 15; voluntary, 130

Alberti, Leon Battista, 51, 52, 53, 54, 55

Alhazen, 11, 43, 45

Al-kindi, 11, 43, 44

Analogy, 66, 112

Angels, 23

Aphrodite, 64

Aristotle, 16, 18, 33–34, 43, 44

Athena, 35, 36, 38, 64, 65

Attention, 10; gathering of, xi

Augustine, 109, 110–111

Aurora, the Dawn, 5

Automatism, 10, 17, 110, 126

Avicenna, 43

Avoidance, ix, viii, 16

Awareness, 20, 41, 81; arrested, 23; cognitive, 109; concentration of, xi; and distinction, 16; embodied, 29, 60; lack of, 59; of light, 102; order of, 29; organic, 90, 126; and poise, 29; receptivity of, 22; as redundancy, 10; refocused, 103; and relation, 101; of resistance, 122; response of, 14; as source of *lumen naturale,* 116; states

of, 115–116; and the stop, 29, 82; time of, 16; of timing, 86

Bacon, Roger, 1, 3, 41, 43, 54, 111

Beckett, Samuel, 29

Berkeley, George, 23–26, 59, 85

Blind man, Descartes's, ix, 19–21, 40–41, 83, 95–99, 115

Blindness: of affection, 8; aversion to, 23; compensation for, 63–65, 77, 79, 96; discovery in, 27; double action of, 5, 6; effect of, 3; enlightened, 11; fixity of, 32; as gift, 77, 78, 102; hysterical, 124; illuminated, 31; impediments of, 13; and knowledge, x, 6; knowledge of the stop in, 26; and language, 72; and light, 3–8; mechanical, 31; and movement, 4, 14; night, 19; oppression in, 95, 96; perception of, 72; philosophical, 14; proof in, 6; as punishment, 3–8, 20, 23–24, 27, 63; pursuit of movement in, 20; redempton through, 11; and reduction of intelligence, 4; revolutionary, 119; as reward, 20; and the sign, 63–75; symbols of, 96; as undemocratic, 4; voluntary, 28

Body: functional aspects, 125; language of, 78; light of, 115–117; luminous, 99; presence in, 78, 79, 101; reengendering, 79; relation to intellect, 135; remembrance in, 132; of sensitivity, 78

The Book of Changes, 88, 89

Boundaries, 74